DAILY

REFLECTIONS

REFLECTIONS

*A
book
of reflections
by A.A. members
for
A.A. members*

www.snowballpublishing.com

info@snowballpublishing.com

For information regarding special discounts for bulk purchases, please contact
Snowball Publishing at

sales@snowballpublishing.com

DAILY
REFLECTIONS

FOREWORD

This volume had its beginning in an Advisory Action of the 1987 General Service Conference, and fulfills a long-felt need in the Fellowship for a collection of reflections that moves through the calendar year—one day at a time.

At the top of each dated page is a quotation from such sources as Bill W. in *Alcoholics Anonymous, Twelve Steps and Twelve Traditions, A.A. Comes of Age, As Bill Sees It,* and *The Best of Bill;* Dr. Bob from *Dr. Bob and the Good Oldtimers;* and other A.A. Conference-approved literature.

Following each quote is a personal reflection, by an individual A.A. member, on the quotation. A request to the entire A.A. Fellowship produced over 1,300 submissions. The A.A. members selected for inclusion are not professional writers, and speak, of course, not for the Fellowship but for themselves—one A.A. member writing to other A.A. members.

As a result of these contributions, the entire book focuses on our Three Legacies of Recovery, Unity and Service, and is in keeping with our Preamble which states that "A.A. is not allied with any sect, denomination, politics, organization or institution."

In his Foreword to *As Bill Sees It,* Bill W. wrote that he hoped that his writings may "become an aid to individual meditation and a stimulant to group discussion, and . . . lead to a still wider reading of all our literature." We can find no more appropriate words to use in introducing this volume of *Daily Reflections.*

"I AM A MIRACLE"

The central fact of our lives today is the absolute certainty that our Creator has entered into our hearts and lives in a way which is indeed miraculous. He has commenced to accomplish those things for us which we could never do by ourselves.

ALCOHOLICS ANONYMOUS, p. 25

This truly is a fact in my life today, and a real miracle. I always believed in God, but could never put that belief meaningfully into my life. Today, because of Alcoholics Anonymous, I now trust and rely on God, as I understand Him; I am sober today because of that! Learning to trust and rely on God was something I could never have done alone. I now believe in miracles because I am one!

FIRST, THE FOUNDATION

Is sobriety all that we can expect of a spiritual awakening? No, sobriety is only a bare beginning.

AS BILL SEES IT, p. 8

Practicing the A.A. program is like building a house. First I had to pour a big, thick concrete slab on which to erect the house; that, to me, was the equivalent of stopping drinking. But it's pretty uncomfortable living on a concrete slab, unprotected and exposed to the heat, cold, wind and rain. So I built a room on the slab by starting to practice the program. The first room was rickety because I wasn't used to the work. But as time passed, as I practiced the program, I learned to build better rooms. The more I practiced, and the more I built, the more comfortable, and happy, was the home I now have to live in.

POWERLESS

We admitted we were powerless over alcohol—that our lives had become unmanageable.
TWELVE STEPS AND TWELVE TRADITIONS, p. 21

It is no coincidence that the very first Step mentions powerlessness: An admission of personal powerlessness over alcohol is a cornerstone of the foundation of recovery. I've learned that I do not have the power and control I once thought I had. I am powerless over what people think about me. I am powerless over having just missed the bus. I am powerless over how other people work (or don't work) the Steps. But I've also learned I am *not* powerless over some things. I am *not* powerless over my attitudes. I am *not* powerless over negativity. I am *not* powerless over assuming responsibility for my own recovery. I have the power to exert a positive influence on myself, my loved ones, and the world in which I live.

BEGIN WHERE YOU ARE

We feel that elimination of our drinking is but a beginning. A much more important demonstration of our principles lies before us in our respective homes, occupations and affairs.

ALCOHOLICS ANONYMOUS, p. 19

It's usually pretty easy for me to be pleasant to the people in an A.A. setting. While I'm working to stay sober, I'm celebrating with my fellow A.A.s our common release from the hell of drinking. It's often not so hard to spread glad tidings to my old and new friends in the program.

At home or at work, though, it can be a different story. It is in situations arising in both of those areas that the little day-to-day frustrations are most evident, and where it can be tough to smile or reach out with a kind word or an attentive ear. It's outside of the A.A. rooms that I face the real test of the effectiveness of my walk through A.A.'s Twelve Steps.

TOTAL ACCEPTANCE

He cannot picture life without alcohol. Some day he will be unable to imagine life either with alcohol or without it. Then he will know loneliness such as few do. He will be at the jumping-off place. He will wish for the end.

ALCOHOLICS ANONYMOUS, p. 152

Only an alcoholic can understand the exact meaning of a statement like this one. The double standard that held me captive as an active alcoholic also filled me with terror and confusion: "If I don't get a drink I'm going to die," competed with "If I continue drinking it's going to kill me." Both compulsive thoughts pushed me ever closer to the bottom. That bottom produced a *total* acceptance of my alcoholism—with no reservations whatsoever—and one that was absolutely essential for my recovery. It was a dilemma unlike anything I had ever faced, but as I found out later on, a necessary one if I was to succeed in this program.

THE VICTORY OF SURRENDER

We perceive that only through utter defeat are we able to take our first steps toward liberation and strength. Our admissions of personal powerlessness finally turn out to be firm bedrock upon which happy and purposeful lives may be built.

TWELVE STEPS AND TWELVE TRADITIONS, p. 21

When alcohol influenced every facet of my life, when bottles became the symbol of all my self-indulgence and permissiveness, when I came to realize that, by myself, I could do nothing to overcome the power of alcohol, I realized I had no recourse except surrender. In surrender I found victory—victory over my selfish self-indulgence, victory over my stubborn resistance to life as it was given to me. When I stopped fighting anybody or anything, I started on the path to sobriety, serenity and peace.

AT THE TURNING POINT

Half measures availed us nothing. We stood at the turning point. We asked His protection and care with complete abandon.

ALCOHOLICS ANONYMOUS, p. 59

Every day I stand at turning points. My thoughts and actions can propel me toward growth or turn me down the road to old habits and to booze. Sometimes turning points are beginnings, as when I decide to start praising, instead of condemning someone. Or when I begin to ask for help instead of going it alone. At other times turning points are endings, such as when I see clearly the need to stop festering resentments or crippling self-seeking. Many shortcomings tempt me daily; therefore, I also have daily opportunities to become aware of them. In one form or another, many of my character defects appear daily: self-condemnation, anger, running away, being prideful, wanting to get even, or acting out of grandiosity.

Attempting half measures to eliminate these defects merely paralyzes my efforts to change. It is only when I ask God for help, with complete abandon, that I become willing—and able—to change.

DO I HAVE A CHOICE?

The fact is that most alcoholics, for reasons yet obscure, have lost the power of choice in drink. Our socalled will power becomes practically nonexistent.
ALCOHOLICS ANONYMOUS, p. 24

My powerlessness over alcohol does not cease when I quit drinking. In sobriety I still have no choice—I can't drink.

The choice I *do have* is to pick up and use the "kit of spiritual tools" (*Alcoholics Anonymous,* p. 25). When I do that, my Higher Power relieves me of my lack of choice—and keeps me sober *one more day.* If I could choose *not to* pick up a drink today, where then would be my need for A.A. or a Higher Power?

AN ACT OF PROVIDENCE

It is truly awful to admit that, glass in hand, we have warped our minds into such an obsession for destructive drinking that only an act of Providence can remove it from us.

TWELVE STEPS AND TWELVE TRADITIONS, p. 21

My act of Providence, (a manifestation of divine care and direction), came as I experienced the total bankruptcy of active alcoholism—everything meaningful in my life was gone. I telephoned Alcoholics Anonymous and, from that instant, my life has never been the same. When I reflect on that very special moment, I know that God was working in my life long before I was able to acknowledge and accept spiritual concepts. The glass was put down through this one act of Providence and my journey into sobriety began. My life continues to unfold with divine care and direction. Step One, in which I admitted I was powerless over alcohol, that my life had become unmanageable, takes on more meaning for me—one day at a time—in the life-saving, life-giving Fellowship of Alcoholics Anonymous.

UNITED WE STAND

We learned that we had to fully concede to our innermost selves that we were alcoholics. This is the first step in recovery. The delusion that we are like other people, or presently may be, has to be smashed.
ALCOHOLICS ANONYMOUS, p. 30

I came to Alcoholics Anonymous because I was no longer able to control my drinking. It was either my wife's complaining about my drinking, or maybe the sheriff forced me to go to A.A. meetings, or perhaps I knew, deep down inside, that I couldn't drink like others, but I was unwilling to admit it because the alternative terrified me. Alcoholics Anonymous is a fellowship of men and women united against a common, fatal disease. Each one of our lives is linked to every other, much like the survivors on a life raft at sea. If we all work together, *we can get safely to shore.*

THE 100% STEP

Only Step One, where we made the 100 percent admission we were powerless over alcohol, can be practiced with absolute perfection.
TWELVE STEPS AND TWELVE TRADITIONS, p. 68

Long before I was able to obtain sobriety in A.A., I knew without a doubt that alcohol was killing me, yet even with this knowledge, I was unable to stop drinking. So, when faced with Step One, I found it easy to admit that I lacked the power to not drink. But was my life unmanageable? Never! Five months after coming into A.A., I was drinking again and wondered why.

Later on, back in A.A. and smarting from my wounds, I learned that Step One is the only Step that can be taken 100%. And that the only way to take it 100% is to take 100% of the Step. That was many twenty-four hours ago and I haven't had to take Step One again.

ACCEPTING OUR PRESENT CIRCUMSTANCES

Our very first problem is to accept our present circumstances as they are, ourselves as we are, and the people about us as they are. This is to adopt a realistic humility without which no genuine advance can even begin. Again and again, we shall need to return to that unflattering point of departure. This is an exercise in acceptance that we can profitably practice every day of our lives.

Provided we strenuously avoid turning these realistic surveys of the facts of life into unrealistic alibis for apathy or defeatism, they can be the sure foundation upon which increased emotional health and therefore spiritual progress can be built.

AS BILL SEES IT, p. 44

When I am having a difficult time accepting people, places or events, I turn to this passage and it relieves me of many an underlying fear regarding others, or situations life presents me. The thought allows me to be human and not perfect, and to regain my peace of mind.

IT DOESN'T HAPPEN OVERNIGHT

We are not cured of alcoholism. What we really have is a daily reprieve contingent on the maintenance of our spiritual condition.
ALCOHOLICS ANONYMOUS, p. 85

The most common alcoholic fantasy seems to be: "If I just don't drink, everything will be all right." Once the fog cleared for me, I saw—for the first time—the mess my life had become. I had family, work, financial and legal problems; I was hung up on old religious ideas; there were sides of my character to which I was inclined to stay blind because they easily could have convinced me that I was hopeless and pushed me toward escape again. The Big Book guided me in resolving *all* of my problems. But it didn't happen overnight—and certainly not automatically—with no effort on my part. I need always to recognize God's mercy and blessings that shine through any problem I have to face.

NO REGRETS

We will not regret the past nor wish to shut the door on it.

ALCOHOLICS ANONYMOUS, p. 83

Once I became sober, I began to see how wasteful my life had been and I experienced overwhelming guilt and feelings of regret. The program's Fourth and Fifth Steps assisted me enormously in healing those troubling regrets. I learned that my self-centeredness and dishonesty stemmed largely from my drinking and that I drank because I was an alcoholic. Now I see how even my most distasteful past experiences can turn to gold because, as a sober alcoholic, I can share them to help my fellow alcoholics, particularly newcomers. Sober for several years in A.A., I no longer regret the past; I am simply grateful to be conscious of God's love and of the help I can give to others in the Fellowship.

AN UNSUSPECTED INNER RESOURCE

With few exceptions our members find that they have tapped an unsuspected inner resource which they presently identify with their own conception of a Power greater than themselves.

ALCOHOLICS ANONYMOUS, pp. 569-70

From my first days in A.A., as I struggled for sobriety, I found hope in these words from our founders. I often pondered the phrase: "they have tapped an unsuspected inner resource." How, I asked myself, can I find the Power within myself, since I am so powerless? In time, as the founders promised, it came to me: I have always had the choice between goodness and evil, between unselfishness and selfishness, between serenity and fear. That Power greater than myself is an original gift that I did not recognize until I achieved daily sobriety through living A.A.'s Twelve Steps.

HITTING BOTTOM

Why all this insistence that every A.A. must hit bottom first? The answer is that few people will sincerely try to practice the A.A. program unless they have hit bottom. For practicing A.A.'s remaining eleven Steps means the adoption of attitudes and actions that almost no alcoholic who is still drinking can dream of taking.

TWELVE STEPS AND TWELVE TRADITIONS, p. 24

Hitting bottom opened my mind and I became willing to try something different. What I tried was A.A. My new life in the Fellowship was a little like learning how to ride a bike for the first time: A.A. became my training wheels *and* my supporting hand. It's not that I wanted the help so much at the time; I simply did not want to hurt like that again. My desire to avoid hitting bottom again was more powerful than my desire to drink. In the beginning that was what kept me sober. But after a while I found myself working the Steps to the best of my ability. I soon realized that my attitudes and actions were changing—if ever so slightly. One Day at a Time, I became comfortable with myself, and others, and my hurting started to heal. Thank God for the training wheels and supporting hand that I choose to call Alcoholics Anonymous.

HAPPINESS COMES QUIETLY

"The trouble with us alcoholics was this: We demanded that the world give us happiness and peace of mind in just the particular order we wanted to get it—by the alcohol route. And we weren't successful. But when we take time to find out some of the spiritual laws, and familiarize ourselves with them, and put them into practice, then we do get happiness and peace of mind. . . . There seem to be some rules that we have to follow, but happiness and peace of mind are always here, open and free to anyone."
DR. BOB AND THE GOOD OLDTIMERS, p. 308

The simplicity of the A.A. program teaches me that happiness isn't something I can "demand." It comes upon me quietly, while I serve others. In offering my hand to the newcomer or to someone who has relapsed, I find that my own sobriety has been recharged with indescribable gratitude and happiness.

WOULD A DRINK HELP?

By going back in our own drinking histories, we could show that years before we realized it we were out of control, that our drinking even then was no mere habit, that it was indeed the beginning of a fatal progression.

TWELVE STEPS AND TWELVE TRADITIONS, p. 23

When I was still drinking, I couldn't respond to any of life's situations the way other, more healthy, people could. The smallest incident triggered a state of mind that believed I had to have a drink to numb my feelings. But the numbing did not improve the situation, so I sought further escape in the bottle. Today I must be aware of my alcoholism. I cannot afford to believe that I have gained control of my drinking—or again I will think I have gained control of my life. Such a feeling of control is fatal to my recovery.

ROUND-THE-CLOCK FAITH

Faith has to work twenty-four hours a day in and through us, or we perish.
ALCOHOLICS ANONYMOUS, p. 16

The essence of my spirituality, and my sobriety, rests on a round-the-clock faith in a Higher Power. I need to remember and rely on the God of my understanding as I pursue all of my daily activities. How comforting for me is the concept that God works in and through people. As I pause in my day, do I recall specific concrete examples of God's presence? Am I amazed and uplifted by the number of times this power is evident? I am overwhelmed with gratitude for my God's presence in my life of recovery. Without this omnipotent force in my every activity, I would again fall into the depths of my disease—and death.

"WE PAUSE . . . AND ASK"

As we go through the day we pause, when agitated or doubtful, and ask for the right thought or action.
ALCOHOLICS ANONYMOUS, p. 87

Today I humbly ask my Higher Power for the grace to find the space between my impulse and my action; to let flow a cooling breeze when I would respond with heat; to interrupt fierceness with gentle peace; to accept the moment which allows judgment to become discernment; to defer to silence when my tongue would rush to attack or defend.

I promise to watch for every opportunity to turn toward my Higher Power for guidance. I know where this power is: it resides within me, as clear as a mountain brook, hidden in the hills—it is the unsuspected Inner Resource.

I thank my Higher Power for this world of light and truth I see when I allow it to direct my vision. I trust it today and hope it trusts me to make all effort to find the right thought or action today.

SERVING MY BROTHER

The member talks to the newcomer not in a spirit of power but in a spirit of humility and weakness.
ALCOHOLICS ANONYMOUS COMES OF AGE p. 279

As the days pass in A.A., I ask God to guide my thoughts and the words that I speak. In this labor of continuous participation in the Fellowship, I have numerous opportunities to speak. So I frequently ask God to help me watch over my thoughts and my words, that they may be the true and proper reflections of our program; to focus my aspirations once again to seek His guidance; to help me be truly kind and loving, helpful and healing, yet always filled with humility, and free from any trace of arrogance.

Today I may very well have to deal with disagreeable attitudes or utterances—the typical stock-in-trade attitude of the still-suffering alcoholic. If this should happen, I will take a moment to center myself in God, so that I will be able to respond from a perspective of composure, strength and sensibility.

"LET'S KEEP IT SIMPLE"

*A few hours later I took my leave of Dr. Bob. . . .
The wonderful, old, broad smile was on his face as
he said almost jokingly, "Remember, Bill, let's not
louse this thing up. Let's keep it simple!" I turned
away, unable to say a word. That was the last time I
ever saw him.*

ALCOHOLICS ANONYMOUS COMES OF AGE, p. 214

After years of sobriety I occasionally ask myself:
"Can it be this simple?" Then, at meetings, I see
former cynics and skeptics who have walked the
A.A. path out of hell by packaging their lives, without alcohol, into twenty-four hour segments, during
which they practice a few principles to the best of
their individual abilities. And then I know again
that, while it isn't always easy, if I keep it simple, it
works.

HAVING FUN YET?

. . . we aren't a glum lot. If newcomers could see no joy or fun in our existence, they wouldn't want it. We absolutely insist on enjoying life. We try not to indulge in cynicism over the state of the nations, nor do we carry the world's troubles on our shoulders.
ALCOHOLICS ANONYMOUS, p. 132

When my own house is in order, I find the different parts of my life are more manageable. Stripped from the guilt and remorse that cloaked my drinking years, I am free to assume my proper role in the universe, but this condition requires maintenance. I should stop and ask myself, *Am I having fun yet?* If I find answering that question difficult or painful, perhaps I'm taking myself too seriously—and finding it difficult to admit that I've strayed from my practice of working the program to keep my house in order. I think the pain I experience is one way my Higher Power has to get my attention, coaxing me to take stock of my performance. The slight time and effort it takes to work the program—a spot-check inventory, for example, or the making of amends, whatever is appropriate—are well worth the effort.

GETTING INVOLVED

There is action and more action. "Faith without works is dead." . . . To be helpful is our only aim.
ALCOHOLICS ANONYMOUS, pp. 88-89

I understand that service is a vital part of recovery but I often wonder, "What can I do?" Simply start with what I have today! I look around to see where there is a need. Are the ashtrays full? Do I have hands and feet to empty them? Suddenly I'm involved! The best speaker may make the worst coffee; the member who's best with newcomers may be unable to read; the one willing to clean up may make a mess of the bank account—yet every one of these people and jobs is essential to an active group. The miracle of service is this: when I use what I have, I find there is more available to me than I realized before.

WHAT WE NEED—EACH OTHER

. . . A.A. is really saying to every serious drinker, "You are an A.A. member if you say so . . . nobody can keep you out."

TWELVE STEPS AND TWELVE TRADITIONS, p. 139

For years, whenever I reflected on Tradition Three ("The only requirement for A.A. membership is a desire to stop drinking"), I thought it valuable only to newcomers. It was their guarantee that no one could bar them from A.A. Today I feel enduring gratitude for the spiritual development the Tradition has brought me. I don't seek out people obviously different from myself. Tradition Three, concentrating on the one way I am similar to others, brought me to know and help every kind of alcoholic, just as they have helped me. Charlotte, the atheist, showed me higher standards of ethics and honor; Clay, of another race, taught me patience; Winslow, who is gay, led me by example into true compassion; Young Megan says that seeing me at meetings, sober thirty years, keeps her coming back. Tradition Three insured that we would get what we need—each other.

RIGOROUS HONESTY

Who wishes to be rigorously honest and tolerant? Who wants to confess his faults to another and make restitution for harm done? Who cares anything about a Higher Power, let alone meditation and prayer? Who wants to sacrifice time and energy in trying to carry A.A.'s message to the next sufferer? No, the average alcoholic, self-centered in the extreme, doesn't care for this prospect—unless he has to do these things in order to stay alive himself.
TWELVE STEPS AND TWELVE TRADITIONS, p. 24

I am an alcoholic. If I drink I will die. My, what power, energy, and emotion this simple statement generates in me! But it's really all I need to know for today. Am I willing to stay alive today? Am I willing to stay sober today? Am I willing to ask for help and am I willing to be a help to another suffering alcoholic today? Have I discovered the fatal nature of my situation? What must I do, today, to stay sober?

FREEDOM FROM GUILT

Where other people were concerned, we had to drop the word "blame" from our speech and thought.
TWELVE STEPS AND TWELVE TRADITIONS, p. 47

When I become willing to accept my own powerlessness, I begin to realize that blaming myself for all the trouble in my life can be an ego trip back into hopelessness. Asking for help and listening deeply to the messages inherent in the Steps and Traditions of the program make it possible to change those attitudes which delay my recovery. Before joining A.A., I had such a desire for approval from people in powerful positions that I was willing to sacrifice myself, and others, to gain a foothold in the world. I invariably came to grief. In the program I find true friends who love, understand, and care to help me learn the truth about myself. With the help of the Twelve Steps, I am able to build a better life, free of guilt and the need for self-justification.

THE TREASURE OF THE PAST

Showing others who suffer how we were given help is the very thing which makes life seem so worth while to us now. Cling to the thought that, in God's hands, the dark past is the greatest possession you have—the key to life and happiness for others. With it you can avert death and misery for them.

ALCOHOLICS ANONYMOUS, p. 124

What a gift it is for me to realize that all those seemingly useless years were not wasted. The most degrading and humiliating experiences turn out to be the most powerful tools in helping others to recover. In knowing the depths of shame and despair, I can reach out with a loving and compassionate hand, and know that the grace of God is available to me.

THE JOY OF SHARING

*Life will take on new meaning. To watch people re-
cover, to see them help others, to watch loneliness
vanish, to see a fellowship grow up about you, to have
a host of friends—this is an experience you must not
miss. We know you will not want to miss it. Frequent
contact with newcomers and with each other is the
bright spot of our lives.*

ALCOHOLICS ANONYMOUS, p. 89

To know that each newcomer with whom I share
has the opportunity to experience the relief that I
have found in this Fellowship fills me with joy and
gratitude. I feel that all the things described in A.A.
will come to pass for them, as they have for me, if
they seize the opportunity and embrace the program fully.

FREEDOM FROM . . . FREEDOM TO

We are going to know a new freedom. . . .
ALCOHOLICS ANONYMOUS, p. 83

Freedom for me is both freedom *from* and freedom *to*. The first freedom I enjoy is freedom from the slavery of alcohol. What a relief! Then I begin to experience freedom *from* fear—fear of people, of economic insecurity, of commitment, of failure, of rejection. Then I begin to enjoy freedom *to*—freedom to *choose* sobriety for today, freedom to be myself, freedom to express my opinion, to experience peace of mind, to love and be loved, and freedom to grow spiritually. But how can I achieve these freedoms? The Big Book clearly says that before I am halfway through making amends, I will begin to know a "new" freedom; not the old freedom of doing what I pleased, without regard to others, but the new freedom that allows fulfillment of the promises in my life. What a joy to be free!

OUR COMMON WELFARE
COMES FIRST

The unity of Alcoholics Anonymous is the most cherished quality our Society has. . . . We stay whole, or A.A. dies.

TWELVE STEPS AND TWELVE TRADITIONS, p. 129

Our Traditions are key elements in the ego deflation process necessary to achieve and maintain sobriety in Alcoholics Anonymous. The First Tradition reminds me not to take credit, or authority, for my recovery. Placing our common welfare first reminds me not to become a healer in this program; I am still one of the patients. Self-effacing elders built the ward. Without it, I doubt I would be alive. Without the group, few alcoholics would recover.

The active role in renewed surrender of will enables me to step aside from the need to dominate, the desire for recognition, both of which played so great a part in my active alcoholism. Deferring my personal desires for the greater good of group growth contributes toward A.A. unity that is central to all recovery. It helps me to remember that the whole is greater than the sum of all its parts.

GOAL: SANITY

". . . Step Two gently and very gradually began to infiltrate my life. I can't say upon what occasion or upon what day I came to believe in a Power greater than myself, but I certainly have that belief now."
TWELVE STEPS AND TWELVE TRADITIONS, p. 27

"Came to believe!" I gave lip service to my belief when I felt like it or when I thought it would look good. I didn't really trust God. I didn't believe He cared for me. I kept trying to change things I couldn't change. Gradually, in disgust, I began to turn it all over, saying: "You're so omnipotent, you take care of it." He did. I began to receive answers to my deepest problems, sometimes at the most unusual times: driving to work, eating lunch, or when I was sound asleep. I realized that I hadn't thought of those solutions—a Power greater than myself had given them to me. I came to believe.

RESCUED BY SURRENDERING

Characteristic of the so-called typical alcoholic is a narcissistic egocentric core, dominated by feelings of omnipotence, intent on maintaining at all costs its inner integrity. . . . Inwardly the alcoholic brooks no control from man or God. He, the alcoholic, is and must be the master of his destiny. He will fight to the end to preserve that position.

A.A. COMES OF AGE, p. 311

The great mystery is: "Why do some of us die alcoholic deaths, fighting to preserve the 'independence' of our ego, while others seem to sober up effortlessly in A. A.?" Help from a Higher Power, the gift of sobriety, came to me when an otherwise unexplained desire to stop drinking coincided with my willingness to accept the suggestions of the men and women of A. A. I had to surrender, for only by reaching out to God and my fellows could I be rescued.

FILLING THE VOID

We needed to ask ourselves but one short question. "Do I now believe, or am I even willing to believe, that there is a Power greater than myself?" As soon as a man can say that he does believe, or is willing to believe, we emphatically assure him that he is on his way.

ALCOHOLICS ANONYMOUS, p. 47

I was always fascinated with the study of scientific principles. I was emotionally and physically distant from people while I pursued Absolute Knowledge. God and spirituality were meaningless academic exercises. I was a modern man of science, knowledge was my Higher Power. Given the right set of equations, life was merely another problem to solve. Yet my inner self was dying from my outer man's solution to life's problems and the solution was alcohol. In spite of my intelligence, alcohol became my Higher Power. It was through the unconditional love which emanated from A.A. people and meetings that I was able to discard alcohol as my Higher Power. The great void was filled. I was no longer lonely and apart from life. I had found a true power greater than myself, I had found God's love. There is only one equation which really matters to me now: God is in A.A.

WHEN FAITH IS MISSING

Sometimes A.A. comes harder to those who have lost or rejected faith than to those who never had any faith at all, for they think they have tried faith and found it wanting. They have tried the way of faith and the way of no faith.

TWELVE STEPS AND TWELVE TRADITIONS, p. 28

I was so sure God had failed me that I became ultimately defiant, though I knew better, and plunged into a final drinking binge. My faith turned bitter and that was no coincidence. Those who once had great faith hit bottom harder. It took time to rekindle my faith, though I came to A.A. I was grateful intellectually to have survived such a great fall, but my heart felt callous. Still, I stuck with the A.A. program; the alternatives were too bleak! I kept coming back and gradually my faith was resurrected.

A GLORIOUS RELEASE

"The minute I stopped arguing, I could begin to see and feel. Right there, Step Two gently and very gradually began to infiltrate my life. I can't say upon what occasion or upon what day I came to believe in a Power greater than myself, but I certainly have that belief now. To acquire it, I had only to stop fighting and practice the rest of A.A.'s program as enthusiastically as I could."

TWELVE STEPS AND TWELVE TRADITIONS, p. 27

After years of indulging in a "self-will run riot," Step Two became for me a glorious release from being all alone. Nothing is so painful or insurmountable in my journey now. Someone is always there to share life's burdens with me. Step Two became a reinforcement with God, and I now realize that my insanity and ego were curiously linked. To rid myself of the former, I must give up the latter to one with far broader shoulders than my own.

A RALLYING POINT

Therefore, Step Two is the rallying point for all of us. Whether agnostic, atheist, or former believer, we can stand together on this Step.
TWELVE STEPS AND TWELVE TRADITIONS, p. 33

I feel that A.A. is a God-inspired program and that God is at every A.A. meeting. I see, believe, and have come to know that A.A. works, because I have stayed sober today. I am turning my life over to A.A. and to God by going to an A.A. meeting. If God is in my heart and everyone else's, then I am a small part of a whole and I am not unique. If God is in my heart and He speaks to me through other people, then I must be a channel of God to other people. I should seek to do His will by living spiritual principles and my reward will be sanity and emotional sobriety.

A PATH TO FAITH

True humility and an open mind can lead us to faith, and every A.A. meeting is an assurance that God will restore us to sanity if we rightly relate ourselves to Him.

TWELVE STEPS AND TWELVE TRADITIONS, p. 33

My last drunk had landed me in the hospital, totally broken. It was then that I was able to see my past float in front of me. I realized that, through drinking, I had lived every nightmare I had ever had. My own self-will and obsession to drink had driven me into a dark pit of hallucinations, blackouts and despair. Finally beaten, I asked for God's help. His presence told me to believe. My obsession for alcohol was taken away and my paranoia has since been lifted. I am no longer afraid. I know my life is healthy and sane.

CONVINCING "MR. HYDE"

Even then, as we hew away, peace and joy will still elude us. That's the place so many of us A.A. oldsters have come to. And it's a hell of a spot, literally. How shall our unconscious—from which so many of our fears, compulsions and phony aspirations still stream —be brought into line with what we actually believe, know and want! How to convince our dumb, raging and hidden "Mr. Hyde" becomes our main task.

THE BEST OF BILL, pp. 42–43

Regular attendance at meetings, serving and helping others is the recipe that many have tried and found to be successful. Whenever I stray from these basic principles, my old habits resurface and my old self also comes back with all its fears and defects. The ultimate goal of each A.A. member is permanent sobriety, achieved One Day at a Time.

GETTING THE "SPIRITUAL ANGLE"

How often do we sit in AA meetings and hear the speaker declare, "But I haven't yet got the spiritual angle." Prior to this statement, he had described a miracle of transformation which had occurred in him—not only his release from alcohol, but a complete change in his whole attitude toward life and the living of it. It is apparent to nearly everyone else present that he has received a great gift; " . . . except that he doesn't seem to know it yet!" We well know that this questioning individual will tell us six months or a year hence that he has found faith in God.

LANGUAGE OF THE HEART, p. 275

A spiritual experience can be the realization that a life which once seemed empty and devoid of meaning is now joyous and full. In my life today, daily prayer and meditation, coupled with living the Twelve Steps, has brought about an inner peace and feeling of belonging which was missing when I was drinking.

I DON'T RUN THE SHOW

When we became alcoholics, crushed by a self-imposed crisis we could not postpone or evade, we had to fearlessly face the proposition that either God is everything or else He is nothing. God either is, or He isn't. What was our choice to be?
ALCOHOLICS ANONYMOUS, p. 53

Today my choice is God. He is everything. For this I am truly grateful. When I think I am running the show I am blocking God from my life. I pray I can remember this when I allow myself to get caught up into self. The most important thing is that today I am willing to grow along spiritual lines, and that God is everything. When I was trying to quit drinking on my own, it never worked; with God and A.A., it is working. This seems to be a simple thought for a complicated alcoholic.

THE LIMITS OF SELF-RELIANCE

We asked ourselves why we had them [fears]. Wasn't it because self-reliance failed us?
ALCOHOLICS ANONYMOUS, p. 68

All of my character defects separate me from God's will. When I ignore my association with Him I face the world and my alcoholism alone and must depend on self-reliance. I have never found security and happiness through self-will and the only result is a life of fear and discontent. God provides the path back to Him and to His gift of serenity and comfort. First, however, I must be willing to acknowledge my fears and understand their source and power over me. I frequently ask God to help me understand how I separate myself from Him.

"THE ROOT OF OUR TROUBLES"

*Selfishness—self-centeredness! That, we think, is the
root of our troubles.*
ALCOHOLICS ANONYMOUS, p. 62

How amazing the revelation that the world, and
everyone in it, can get along just fine with or without me. What a relief to know that people, places
and things will be perfectly okay without my control and direction. And how wordlessly wonderful
to come to believe that a power greater than me
exists separate and apart from myself. I believe that
the feeling of separation I experience between me
and God will one day vanish. In the meantime,
faith must serve as the pathway to the center of my
life.

WE CAN'T THINK OUR WAY SOBER

To the intellectually self-sufficient man or woman, many A.A.'s can say, "Yes, we were like you—far too smart for our own good. . . . Secretly, we felt we could float above the rest of the folks on our brain power alone."

AS BILL SEES IT, p. 60

Even the most brilliant mind is no defense against the disease of alcoholism. I can't think my way sober. I try to remember that intelligence is a God-given attribute that I may use, a joy—like having a talent for dancing or drawing or carpentry. It does not make me better than anyone else, and it is not a particularly reliable tool for recovery, for it is a power greater than myself who will restore me to sanity—not a high IQ or a college degree.

EXPECTATIONS vs. DEMANDS

Burn the idea into the consciousness of every man that he can get well regardless of anyone. The only condition is that he trust in God and clean house.

ALCOHOLICS ANONYMOUS, p. 98

Dealing with expectations is a frequent topic at meetings. It isn't wrong to expect progress of myself, good things from life, or decent treatment from others. Where I get into trouble is when my expectations become demands. I will fall short of what I wish to be and situations will go in ways I do not like, because people will let me down sometimes. The only question is: "What am I going to do about it?" Wallow in self-pity or anger; retaliate and make a bad situation worse; or will I trust in God's power to bring blessings on the messes in which I find myself? Will I ask Him what I should be learning; do I keep on doing the right things I know how to do, no matter what; do I take time to share my faith and blessings with others?

TAKING ACTION

Are these extravagant promises? We think not. They are being fulfilled among us—sometimes quickly, sometimes slowly. They will always materialize if we work for them.

ALCOHOLICS ANONYMOUS, p. 84

One of the most important things A.A. has given me, in addition to freedom from booze, is the ability to take "right action." It says the promises will *always* materialize if I *work* for them. Fantasizing about them, debating them, preaching about them and faking them just won't work. I'll remain a miserable, rationalizing dry drunk. By taking action and working the Twelve Steps in all my affairs, I'll have a life beyond my wildest dreams.

COMMITMENT

Understanding is the key to right principles and attitudes, and right action is the key to good living.
TWELVE STEPS AND TWELVE TRADITIONS, p. 125

There came a time in my program of recovery when the third stanza of the Serenity Prayer—"The wisdom to know the difference"—became indelibly imprinted in my mind. From that time on, I had to face the ever-present knowledge that my every action, word and thought was within, or outside, the principles of the program. I could no longer hide behind self-rationalization, nor behind the insanity of my disease. The only course open to me, if I was to attain a joyous life for myself (and subsequently for those I love), was one in which I imposed on myself an effort of commitment, discipline, and responsibility.

THE LOVE IN THEIR EYES

Some of us won't *believe in God, others can't, and still others who do believe that God exists have no faith whatever He will perform this miracle.*
TWELVE STEPS AND TWELVE TRADITIONS, p. 25

It was the changes I saw in the new people who came into the Fellowship that helped me lose my fear, and change my negative attitude to a positive one. I could see the love in their eyes and I was impressed by how much their "One Day at a Time" sobriety meant to them. They had looked squarely at Step Two and came to believe that a power greater than themselves was restoring them to sanity. That gave me faith in the Fellowship, and hope that it could work for me too. I found that God was a loving God, not that punishing God I feared before coming to A.A. I also found that He had been with me during all those times I had been in trouble before I came to A.A. I know today that He was the one who led me to A.A. and that I am a miracle.

OUR PATHS ARE OUR OWN

*. . . there was nothing left for us but to pick up the
simple kit of spiritual tools laid at our feet.*
ALCOHOLICS ANONYMOUS, p. 25

My first attempt at the Steps was one of obligation
and necessity, which resulted in a deep feeling of
discouragement in the face of all those adverbs:
courageously; completely; humbly; directly; and
only. I considered Bill W. fortunate to have gone
through such a major, even sensational, spiritual
experience. I had to discover, as time went on, that
my path was my own. After a few twenty-four
hours in the A.A. Fellowship, thanks especially to
the sharing of members in the meetings, I understood that everyone gradually finds his or her own
pace in moving through the Steps. Through progressive means, I try to live according to these suggested principles. As a result of these Steps, I can
say today that my attitude towards life, people, and
towards anything having to do with God, has been
transformed and improved.

I'M NOT DIFFERENT

In the beginning, it was four whole years before A.A. brought permanent sobriety to even one alcoholic woman. Like the "high bottoms," the women said they were different; . . . The Skid-Rower said he was different . . . so did the artists and the professional people, the rich, the poor, the religious, the agnostic, the Indians and the Eskimos, the veterans, and the prisoners. . . . nowadays all of these, and legions more, soberly talk about how very much alike all of us alcoholics are when we admit that the chips are finally down.

AS BILL SEES IT, p. 24

I cannot consider myself "different" in A.A.; if I do I isolate myself from others and from contact with my Higher Power. If I feel isolated in A.A., it is not something for which others are responsible. It is something I've created by feeling I'm "different" in some way. Today I practice being just another alcoholic in the worldwide Fellowship of Alcoholics Anonymous.

THE GIFT OF LAUGHTER

At this juncture, his A.A. sponsor usually laughs.
TWELVE STEPS AND TWELVE TRADITIONS, p. 26

Before my recovery from alcoholism began, laughter was one of the most painful sounds I knew. I never laughed and I felt that anyone else's laughter was directed at me! My self-pity and anger denied me the simplest of pleasures or lightness of heart. By the end of my drinking not even alcohol could provoke a drunken giggle in me.

When my A.A. sponsor began to laugh and point out my self-pity and ego-feeding deceptions, I was annoyed and hurt, but it taught me to lighten up and focus on my recovery. I soon learned to laugh at myself and eventually I taught those I sponsor to laugh also. Every day I ask God to help me stop taking myself too seriously.

I'M PART OF THE WHOLE

At once, I became a part—if only a tiny part—of a cosmos. . . .

AS BILL SEES IT, p. 225

When I first came to A.A., I decided that "they" were very nice people—perhaps a little naive, a little too friendly, but basically decent, earnest people (with whom I had nothing in common). I saw "them" at meetings—after all, that was where "they" existed. I shook hands with "them" and, when I went out the door, I forgot about "them."

Then one day my Higher Power, whom I did not then believe in, arranged to create a community project outside of A.A., but one which happened to involve many A.A. members. We worked together, I got to know "them" as people. I came to admire "them," even to like "them" and, in spite of myself, to enjoy "them." "Their" practice of the program in their daily lives—not just in talk at meetings—attracted me and I wanted what they had. Suddenly the "they" became "we." I have not had a drink since.

GUIDANCE

. . . this means a belief in a Creator who is all power, justice, and love; a God who intends for me a purpose, a meaning, and a destiny to grow, however . . . haltingly, toward His own likeness and image.
AS BILL SEES IT, p. 51

As I began to understand my own powerlessness and my dependence on God, as I understand Him, I began to see that there was a life which, if I could have it, I would have chosen for myself from the beginning. It is through the continuing work of the Steps and the life in the Fellowship that I've learned to see that there is truly a better way into which I am being guided. As I come to know more about God, I am able to trust His ways and His plans for the development of His character in me. Quickly or not so quickly, I grow toward His own image and likeness.

MYSTERIOUS PARADOXES

Such is the paradox of A.A. regeneration: strength arising out of complete defeat and weakness, the loss of one's old life as a condition for finding a new one.
A.A. COMES OF AGE, p. 46

What glorious mysteries paradoxes are! They do not compute, yet when recognized and accepted, they reaffirm something in the universe beyond human logic. When I face a fear, I am given courage; when I support a brother or sister, my capacity to love myself is increased; when I accept pain as part of the growing experience of life, I realize a greater happiness; when I look at my dark side, I am brought into new light; when I accept my vulnerabilities and surrender to a Higher Power, I am graced with unforeseen strength. I stumbled through the doors of A.A. in disgrace, expecting nothing from life, and I have been given hope and dignity. Miraculously, the only way to keep the gifts of the program is to pass them on.

A THANKFUL HEART

I try to hold fast to the truth that a full and thankful heart cannot entertain great conceits. When brimming with gratitude, one's heartbeat must surely result in outgoing love, the finest emotion that we can ever know.

AS BILL SEES IT, p. 37

My sponsor told me that I should be a grateful alcoholic and always have "an attitude of gratitude"—that gratitude was the basic ingredient of humility, that humility was the basic ingredient of anonymity and that "anonymity was the spiritual foundation of all our Traditions, ever reminding us to place principles before personalities." As a result of this guidance, I start every morning on my knees, thanking God for three things: I'm alive, I'm sober, and I'm a member of Alcoholics Anonymous. Then I try to live an "attitude of gratitude" and thoroughly enjoy another twenty-four hours of the A.A. way of life. A.A. is not something I joined; it's something I live.

THE CHALLENGE OF FAILURE

In God's economy, nothing is wasted. Through failure, we learn a lesson in humility which is probably needed, painful though it is.

AS BILL SEES IT, p. 31

How thankful I am today, to know that *all* my past failures were necessary for me to be where I am now. Through much pain came experience and, in suffering, I became obedient. When I sought God, as I understand Him, He shared His treasured gifts. Through experience and obedience, growth started, followed by gratitude. Yes, then came peace of mind—living in and sharing sobriety.

NO ORDINARY SUCCESS STORY

A.A. is no success story in the ordinary sense of the word. It is a story of suffering transmuted, under grace, into spiritual progress.

AS BILL SEES IT, p. 35

Upon entering A.A. I listened to others talk about the reality of their drinking: loneliness, terror and pain. As I listened further, I soon heard a description of a very different kind—the reality of sobriety. It is a reality of freedom and happiness, of purpose and direction, and of serenity and peace with God, ourselves and others. By attending meetings I am reintroduced to that reality, over and over. I see it in the eyes and hear it in the voices of those around me. By working the program I find the direction and strength with which to make it mine. The joy of A.A. is that this new reality is available to me.

A UNIQUE STABILITY

Where does A.A. get its direction? . . . These practical folk then read Tradition Two, and learn that the sole authority in A.A. is a loving God as He may express Himself in the group conscience. . . . The elder statesman is the one who sees the wisdom of the group's decision, who holds no resentment over his reduced status, whose judgment, fortified by considerable experience, is sound, and who is willing to sit quietly on the sidelines patiently awaiting developments.

TWELVE STEPS AND TWELVE TRADITIONS, pp. 132, 135

Into the fabric of recovery from alcoholism are woven the Twelve Steps and the Twelve Traditions. As my recovery progressed, I realized that the new mantle was tailor-made for me. The elders of the group gently offered suggestions when change seemed impossible. Everyone's shared experiences became the substance for treasured friendships. I know that the Fellowship is ready and equipped to aid each suffering alcoholic at all crossroads in life. In a world beset by many problems, I find this assurance a unique stability. I cherish the gift of sobriety. I offer God my gratitude for the strength I receive in a Fellowship that truly exists for the good of all members.

WHAT? NO PRESIDENT?

When told that our Society has no president having authority to govern it, no treasurer who can compel the payment of any dues, . . . our friends gasp and exclaim, "This simply can't be. . . ."
TWELVE STEPS AND TWELVE TRADITIONS, p. 132

When I finally made my way to A.A., I could not believe that there was no treasurer to "compel the payment of dues." I could not imagine an organization that didn't require monetary contributions in return for a service. It was my first and, thus far, only experience with getting "something for nothing." Because I did not feel used or conned by those in A.A., I was able to approach the program free from bias and with an open mind. They wanted nothing from me. What could I lose? I thank God for the wisdom of the early founders who knew so well the alcoholic's disdain for being manipulated.

ONE A.A. MIRACLE

Save for a few brief moments of temptation the thought of drink has never returned; and at such times a great revulsion has risen up in him. Seemingly he could not drink even if he would. God had restored his sanity.

ALCOHOLICS ANONYMOUS, p. 57

The word "God" was frightening to me when I first saw it associated with A.A.'s Twelve Steps. Having tried all the means I could to stop drinking, I found that it was not possible for me to sustain that desire over a period of time. Yet, how could I believe in a "God" that had allowed me to sink to the deep despair that engulfed me—whether drinking or dry?

The answer was in finally admitting that it *might* be possible for me to know the mercy of a Power greater than myself who could grant me sobriety contingent on my willingness to "come to believe." By finally admitting that I was one among many, and by following the example of my sponsor and other A.A. members in practicing faith I did not have, my life has been given meaning, direction and purpose.

IT WORKS

It works—it really does.
ALCOHOLICS ANONYMOUS, p. 88

When I got sober I initially had faith only in the program of Alcoholics Anonymous. Desperation and fear kept me sober (and maybe a caring and/or tough sponsor helped!). Faith in a Higher Power came much later. This faith came slowly at first, after I began listening to others share at meetings about their experiences—experiences that I had never faced sober, but that they were facing with strength from a Higher Power. Out of their sharing came hope that I too would—and could—"get" a Higher Power. In time, I learned that a Higher Power—a faith that works under all conditions—is possible. Today this faith, plus the honesty, open-mindedness and willingness to work the Steps of the program, gives me the serenity that I seek. It works—it really does.

HOPE

Do not be discouraged.
ALCOHOLICS ANONYMOUS, p. 60

Few experiences are of less value to me than fast sobriety. Too many times discouragement has been the bonus for unrealistic expectations, not to mention self-pity or fatigue from my wanting to change the world by the weekend. Discouragement is a warning signal that I may have wandered across the God line. The secret of fulfilling my potential is in acknowledging my limitations and believing that time is a gift, not a threat.

Hope is the key that unlocks the door of discouragement. The program promises me that if I do not pick up the first drink today, I will always have hope. Having come to believe that I keep what I share, every time I encourage, I receive courage. It is with others that, with the grace of God and the Fellowship of A.A., I trudge the road of happy destiny. May I always remember that the power within me is far greater than any fear before me. May I always have patience, for I am on the right road.

OVERCOMING SELF-WILL

So our troubles, we think, are basically of our own making. They arise out of ourselves, and the alcoholic is an extreme example of self-will run riot, though he usually doesn't think so. Above everything, we alcoholics must be rid of this selfishness. We must, or it kills us!

ALCOHOLICS ANONYMOUS, p. 62

For so many years my life revolved solely around myself. I was consumed with self in all forms—self-centeredness, self-pity, self-seeking, all of which stemmed from pride. Today I have been given the gift, through the Fellowship of Alcoholics Anonymous, of practicing the Steps and Traditions in my daily life, of my group and sponsor, and the capacity—if I so choose—to put my pride aside in all situations which arise in my life.

Until I could honestly look at myself and see that I was the problem in many situations and react appropriately inside and out; until I could discard my expectations and understand that my serenity was directly proportional to them, I could not experience serenity and sound sobriety.

WEEDING THE GARDEN

The essence of all growth is a willingness to make a change for the better and then an unremitting willingness to shoulder whatever responsibility this entails.

AS BILL SEES IT, p. 115

By the time I had reached Step Three I had been freed of my dependence on alcohol, but bitter experience has shown me that continuous sobriety requires continuous effort.

Every now and then I pause to take a good look at my progress. More and more of my garden is weeded each time I look, but each time I also find new weeds sprouting where I thought I had made my final pass with the blade. As I head back to get the newly sprouted weed (it's easier when they are young), I take a moment to admire how lush the growing vegetables and flowers are, and my labors are rewarded. My sobriety grows and bears fruit.

A LIFELONG TASK

"But just how, in these circumstances, does a fellow 'take it easy?' That's what I want to know."
TWELVE STEPS AND TWELVE TRADITIONS, p. 26

I was never known for my patience. How many times have I asked, "Why should I wait, when I can have it all right now?" Indeed, when I was first presented the Twelve Steps, I was like the proverbial "kid in a candy store." I couldn't wait to get to Step Twelve; it was surely just a few months' work, or so I thought! I realize now that living the Twelve Steps of A.A. is a lifelong undertaking.

THE IDEA OF FAITH

Do not let any prejudice you may have against spiritual terms deter you from honestly asking yourself what they mean to you.
ALCOHOLICS ANONYMOUS, p. 47

The idea of faith is a very large chunk to swallow when fear, doubt and anger abound in and around me. Sometimes just the idea of doing something different, something I am not accustomed to doing, can eventually become an act of faith if I do it regularly, and do it without debating whether it's the right thing to do. When a bad day comes along and everything is going wrong, a meeting or a talk with another drunk often distracts me just enough to persuade me that everything is not quite as impossible, as overwhelming as I had thought. In the same way, going to a meeting or talking to a fellow alcoholic are acts of faith; I believe I'm arresting my disease. These are ways I slowly move toward faith in a Higher Power.

THE KEY IS WILLINGNESS

Once we have placed the key of willingness in the lock and have the door ever so slightly open, we find that we can always open it some more.
TWELVE STEPS AND TWELVE TRADITIONS, p. 35

The willingness to give up my pride and self-will to a Power greater than myself has proved to be the only ingredient absolutely necessary to solve all of my problems today. Even the smallest amount of willingness, if sincere, is sufficient to allow God to enter and take control over any problem, pain, or obsession. My level of comfort is in direct relation to the degree of willingness I possess at any given moment to give up my self-will, and allow God's will to be manifested in my life. With the key of willingness, my worries and fears are powerfully transformed into serenity.

TURNING IT OVER

Every man and woman who has joined A.A. and intends to stick has, without realizing it, made a beginning on Step Three. Isn't it true that in all matters touching upon alcohol, each of them has decided to turn his or her life over to the care, protection, and guidance of Alcoholics Anonymous? . . . Any willing newcomer feels sure A.A. is the only safe harbor for the foundering vessel he has become. Now if this is not turning one's will and life over to a newfound Providence, then what is it?

TWELVE STEPS AND TWELVE TRADITIONS, p. 35

Submission to God was the first step to my recovery. I believe our Fellowship seeks a spirituality open to a new kinship with God. As I exert myself to follow the path of the Steps, I sense a freedom that gives me the ability to think for myself. My addiction confined me without any release and hindered my ability to be released from my self-confinement, but A.A. assures me of a way to go forward. Mutual sharing, concern and caring for others is our natural gift to each other and mine is strengthened as my attitude toward God changes. I learn to submit to God's will in my life, to have self-respect, and to keep both of these attitudes by giving away what I receive.

SURRENDERING SELF-WILL

Made a decision to turn our will and our lives over to the care of God as we understood Him.
TWELVE STEPS AND TWELVE TRADITIONS, p. 34

No matter how much one wishes to try, exactly how can one turn his own will and his own life over to the care of whatever God he thinks there is? In my search for the answer to this question, I became aware of the wisdom with which it was written: that this is a two-part Step.

I could see many times where I should have died, or at least been injured, during my previous style of living, and it never happened. Someone, or something, was looking after me. I choose to believe my life has always been in God's care. He alone controls the number of days I will be granted until physical death.

The matter of will (self-will or God's will) is the more difficult part of the Step for me. It is only when I have experienced enough emotional pain, through failed attempts to fix myself, that I become willing to surrender to God's will for my life. Surrender is like the calm after the storm. When my will is in line with God's will for me, there is peace within.

TODAY, IT'S MY CHOICE

. . . we invariably find that at some time in the past we have made decisions based on self which later placed us in a position to be hurt.

ALCOHOLICS ANONYMOUS, p. 62

With the realization and acceptance that I had played a part in the way my life had turned out came a dramatic change in my outlook. It was at this point that the A.A. program began to work for me. In the past I had always blamed others, either God or other people, for my circumstances. I never felt that I had a choice in altering my life. My decisions had been based on fear, pride, or ego. As a result, those decisions led me down a path of self-destruction. Today I try to allow my God to guide me on the road to sanity. I am responsible for my action—or inaction—whatever the consequences may be.

GOOD ORDERLY DIRECTION

It is when we try to make our will conform with God's that we begin to use it rightly. To all of us, this was a most wonderful revelation. Our whole trouble had been the misuse of willpower. We had tried to bombard our problems with it instead of attempting to bring it into agreement with God's intention for us. *To make this increasingly possible is the purpose of A.A.'s Twelve Steps, and Step Three opens the door.*

TWELVE STEPS AND TWELVE TRADITIONS, p. 40

All I have to do is look back at my past to see where my self-will has led me. I just don't know what's best for me and I believe my Higher Power does. G.O.D., which I define as "Good Orderly Direction," has never let me down, but I have let myself down quite often. Using my self-will in a situation usually has the same result as forcing the wrong piece into a jigsaw puzzle—exhaustion and frustration.

Step Three opens the door to the rest of the program. When I ask God for guidance I know that whatever happens is the best possible situation, things are exactly as they are supposed to be, even if they aren't what I want or expect. God *does* do for me what I cannot do for myself, if I let Him.

A DAY'S PLAN

On awakening let us think about the twenty-four hours ahead. We consider our plans for the day. Before we begin, we ask God to direct our thinking, especially asking that it be divorced from self-pity, dishonest or self-seeking motives.
ALCOHOLICS ANONYMOUS, p. 86

Every day I ask God to kindle within me the fire of His love, so that love, burning bright and clear, will illuminate my thinking and permit me to better do His will. Throughout the day, as I allow outside circumstances to dampen my spirits, I ask God to sear my consciousness with the awareness that I can start my day over any time I choose; a hundred times, if necessary.

A WORLD OF THE SPIRIT

We have entered the world of the Spirit. Our next function is to grow in understanding and effectiveness. This is not an overnight matter. It should continue for our lifetime.

ALCOHOLICS ANONYMOUS, p. 84

The word "entered" . . . and the phrase "entered into the world of the Spirit" are very significant. They imply action, a beginning, getting into, a prerequisite to maintaining my spiritual growth, the "Spirit" being the immaterial part of me. Barriers to my spiritual growth are self-centeredness and a materialistic focus on wordly things. Spirituality means devotion to spiritual instead of wordly things, it means obedience to God's will for me. I understand spiritual things to be: unconditional love, joy, patience, kindness, goodness, faithfulness, self-control and humility. Any time I allow selfishness, dishonesty, resentment and fear to be a part of me, I block out spiritual things. As I maintain my sobriety, growing spiritually becomes a lifelong process. My goal is spiritual growth, accepting that I'll never have spiritual perfection.

THE KEYSTONE

He is the Father, and we are His children. Most good ideas are simple, and this concept was the keystone of the new and triumphant arch through which we passed to freedom.

ALCOHOLICS ANONYMOUS, p. 62

A keystone is the wedge-shaped piece at the highest part of an arch that locks the other pieces in place. The "other pieces" are Steps One, Two, and Four through Twelve. In one sense this sounds like Step Three is the most important Step, that the other eleven depend on the third for support. In reality however, Step Three is just one of twelve. It is the keystone, but without eleven other stones to build the base and arms, keystone or not, there will be no arch. Through daily working of all Twelve Steps, I find that triumphant arch waiting for me to pass through to another day of freedom.

THE GOD IDEA

When we saw others solve their problems by a simple reliance upon the Spirit of the Universe, we had to stop doubting the power of God. Our ideas did not work. But the God idea did.
ALCOHOLICS ANONYMOUS, p. 52

Like a blind man gradually being restored to sight, I slowly groped my way to the Third Step. Having realized that only a Power greater than myself could rescue me from the hopeless abyss I was in, I knew that this was a Power that I had to grasp, and that it would be my anchor in the midst of a sea of woes. Even though my faith at that time was minuscule, it was big enough to make me see that it was time for me to discard my reliance on my prideful ego and replace it with the steadying strength that could only come from a Power far greater than myself.

AS WE UNDERSTAND HIM

My friend suggested what then seemed a novel idea. . . . "Why don't you choose your own conception of God?" *That statement hit me hard. It melted the icy intellectual mountain in whose shadow I had lived and shivered many years. I stood in the sunlight at last.* It was only a matter of being willing to believe in a Power greater than myself. Nothing more was required of me to make my beginning.

ALCOHOLICS ANONYMOUS, p. 12

I remember the times I looked up into the sky and reflected on who started it all, and how. When I came to A.A., an understanding of some description of the spiritual dimension became a necessary adjunct to a stable sobriety. After reading a variety of versions, including the scientific, of a great explosion, I went for simplicity and made the God of my understanding the Great Power that made the explosion possible. With the vastness of the universe under His command, He would, no doubt, be able to guide my thinking and actions if I was prepared to accept His guidance. But I could not expect help if I turned my back on that help and went my own way. I became willing to believe and I have had 26 years of stable and satisfying sobriety.

MYSTERIOUS WAYS

. . . out of every season of grief or suffering, when the hand of God seemed heavy or even unjust, new lessons for living were learned, new resources of courage were uncovered, and that finally, inescapably, the conviction came that God does "move in a mysterious way His wonders to perform."
TWELVE STEPS AND TWELVE TRADITIONS, p. 105

After losing my career, family and health, I remained unconvinced that my way of life needed a second look. My drinking and other drug use were killing me, but I had never met a recovering person or an A.A. member. I thought I was destined to die alone and that I deserved it. At the peak of my despair, my infant son became critically ill with a rare disease. Doctors' efforts to help him proved useless. I redoubled my efforts to block my feelings, but now the alcohol had stopped working. I was left staring into God's eyes, begging for help. My introduction to A.A. came within days, through an odd series of coincidences, and I have remained sober ever since. My son lived and his disease is in remission. The entire episode convinced me of my powerlessness and the unmanageability of my life. Today my son and I thank God for His intervention.

REAL INDEPENDENCE

The more we become willing to depend upon a Higher Power, the more independent we actually are.

TWELVE STEPS AND TWELVE TRADITIONS, p. 36

I start with a little willingness to trust God and He causes that willingness to grow. The more willingness I have, the more trust I gain, and the more trust I gain, the more willingness I have. My dependence on God grows as my trust in Him grows. Before I became willing, I depended on myself for all my needs and I was restricted by my incompleteness. Through my willingness to depend upon my Higher Power, whom I choose to call God, all my needs are provided for by Someone Who knows me better than I know myself—even the needs I may not realize, as well as the ones yet to come. Only Someone Who knows me that well could bring me to be myself and to help me fill the need in someone else that only I am meant to fill. There never will be another exactly like me. And that is real independence.

PRAYER: IT WORKS

It has been well said that "almost the only scoffers at prayer are those who never tried it enough."
TWELVE STEPS AND TWELVE TRADITIONS, p. 97

Having grown up in an agnostic household, I felt somewhat foolish when I first tried praying. I knew there was a Higher Power working in my life—how else was I staying sober?—but I certainly wasn't convinced he/she/it wanted to hear my prayers. People who had what I wanted said prayer was an important part of practicing the program, so I persevered. With a commitment to daily prayer, I was amazed to find myself becoming more serene and comfortable with my place in the world. In other words, life became easier and less of a struggle. I'm still not sure who, or what, listens to my prayers, but I'd never stop saying them for the simple reason that they work.

LOVE AND TOLERANCE

Love and tolerance of others is our code.
ALCOHOLICS ANONYMOUS, p. 84

I have found that I have to forgive others in all situations to maintain any real spiritual progress. The vital importance of forgiving may not be obvious to me at first sight, but my studies tell me that every great spiritual teacher has insisted strongly upon it.

I must forgive injuries, not just in words, or as a matter of form, but in my heart. I do this not for the other persons' sake, but for my own sake. Resentment, anger, or a desire to see someone punished, are things that rot my soul. Such things fasten my troubles to me with chains. They tie me to other problems that have nothing to do with my original problem.

MATERIAL AND SPIRITUAL
WELL-BEING

Fear . . . of economic insecurity will leave us.
ALCOHOLICS ANONYMOUS, p. 84

Having fear reduced or eliminated and having economic circumstances improve, are two different things. When I was new in A.A., I had those two ideas confused. I thought fear would leave me only when I started making money. However, another line from the Big Book jumped off the page one day when I was chewing on my financial difficulties: "For us, material well-being always followed spiritual progress; it never preceded." (p. 127). I suddenly understood that this promise was a guarantee. I saw that it put priorities in the correct order, that spiritual progress would diminish that terrible fear of being destitute, just as it diminished many other fears.

Today I try to use the talents God gave me to benefit others. I've found that is what others valued all along. I try to remember that I no longer work for myself. I only get the use of the wealth God created, I never have "owned" it. My life's purpose is much clearer when I just work to help, not to possess.

NO MORE STRUGGLE. . .

*And we have ceased fighting anything or anyone—
even alcohol.*

ALCOHOLICS ANONYMOUS, p. 84

When A.A. found me, I thought I was in for a struggle, and that A.A. might provide the strength I needed to beat alcohol. Victorious in that fight, who knows what other battles I could win. I would need to be strong, though. All my previous experience with life proved that. Today I do not have to struggle or exert my will. If I take those Twelve Steps and let my Higher Power do the real work, my alcohol problem disappears all by itself. My living problems also cease to be struggles. I just have to ask whether acceptance—or change—is required. It is not my will, but His, that needs doing.

. . . AND NO MORE RESERVATIONS

We have seen the truth again and again: "Once an alcoholic, always an alcoholic." . . . *If we are planning to stop drinking, there must be no reservation of any kind, nor any lurking notion that someday we will be immune to alcohol.* . . . *To be gravely affected, one does not necessarily have to drink a long time nor take the quantities some of us have. This is particularly true of women. Potential female alcoholics often turn into the real thing and are gone beyond recall in a few years.*

ALCOHOLICS ANONYMOUS, p. 33

These words are underlined in my book. They are true for men and women alcoholics. On many occasions I've turned to this page and reflected on this passage. I need never fool myself by recalling my sometimes differing drinking patterns, or by believing I am "cured." I like to think that, if sobriety is God's gift to me, then my sober life is my gift to God. I hope God is as happy with His gift as I am with mine.

ACTIVE, NOT PASSIVE

Man is supposed to think, and act. He wasn't made in God's image to be an automaton.

AS BILL SEES IT, p. 55

Before I joined A.A., I often did not think, and reacted to people and situations. When not reacting I acted in a mechanical fashion. After joining A.A., I started seeking daily guidance from a Power greater than myself, and learning to listen for that guidance. Then I began to make decisions and act on them, rather than react to them. The results have been constructive; I no longer allow others to make decisions for me and then criticize me for it.

Today—and every day—with a heart full of gratitude, and a desire for God's will to be done through me, my life is worth sharing, especially with my fellow alcoholics! Above all, if I do not make a religion out of anything, even A.A., then I can be an open channel for God's expression.

A FULL AND THANKFUL HEART

I try hard to hold fast to the truth that a full and thankful heart cannot entertain great conceits. When brimming with gratitude, one's heartbeat must surely result in outgoing love, the finest emotion that we can ever know.

AS BILL SEES IT, p. 37

I believe that we in Alcoholics Anonymous are fortunate in that we are constantly reminded of the need to be grateful and of how important gratitude is to our sobriety. I am truly grateful for the sobriety God has given me through the A.A. program and am glad I can give back what was given to me freely. I am grateful not only for sobriety, but for the quality of life my sobriety has brought. God has been gracious enough to give me sober days *and* a life blessed with peace and contentment, as well as the ability to give and receive love, and the opportunity to serve others—in our Fellowship, my family and my community. For all of this, I have "a full and thankful heart."

THE TEACHING IS NEVER OVER

Abandon yourself to God as you understand God. Admit your faults to Him and to your fellows. Clear away the wreckage of your past. Give freely of what you find and join us. We shall be with you in the Fellowship of the Spirit, and you will surely meet some of us as you trudge the Road of Happy Destiny. May God bless you and keep you—until then.
                              ALCOHOLICS ANONYMOUS, p. 164

These words put a lump in my throat each time I read them. In the beginning it was because I felt, "Oh no! The teaching is over. Now I'm on my own. It will never be this new again." Today I feel deep affection for our A.A. pioneers when I read this passage, realizing that it sums up all of what I believe in, and strive for, and that—with God's blessing—the teaching is never over, I'm never on my own, and every day is brand new.

A.A.'s FREEDOMS

We trust that we already know what our several freedoms truly are; that no future generation of AAs will ever feel compelled to limit them. Our AA freedoms create the soil in which genuine love can grow. . . .
LANGUAGE OF THE HEART, p. 303

I craved freedom. First, freedom to drink; later, freedom from drink. The A.A. program of recovery rests on a foundation of free choice. There are no mandates, laws or commandments. A.A.'s spiritual program, as outlined in the Twelve Steps, and by which I am offered even greater freedoms, is only suggested. I can take it or leave it. Sponsorship is offered, not forced, and I come and go as I will. It is these and other freedoms that allow me to recapture the dignity that was crushed by the burden of drink, and which is so dearly needed to support an enduring sobriety.

EQUALITY

Our membership ought to include all who suffer from alcoholism. Hence we may refuse none who wish to recover. Nor ought A.A. membership ever depend upon money or conformity. Any two or three alcoholics gathered together for sobriety may call themselves an A.A. group, provided that, as a group, they have no other affiliation.

ALCOHOLICS ANONYMOUS, p. 565

Prior to A.A., I often felt that I didn't "fit in" with the people around me. Usually "they" had more/less money than I did, and my points of view didn't jibe with "theirs." The amount of prejudice I had experienced in society only proved to me just how phony some self-righteous people were. After joining A.A., I found the way of life I had been searching for. In A.A. no member is better than any other member; we're just alcoholics trying to recover from alcoholism.

TRUSTED SERVANTS

They are servants. Theirs is the sometimes thankless privilege of doing the group's chores.
TWELVE STEPS AND TWELVE TRADITIONS, p. 134

In *Zorba the Greek*, Nikos Kazantzakis describes an encounter between his principal character and an old man busily at work planting a tree. "What is it you are doing?" Zorba asks. The old man replies: "You can see very well what I'm doing, my son, I'm planting a tree." "But why plant a tree," Zorba asks, "if you won't be able to see it bear fruit?" And the old man answers: "I, my son, live as though I were never going to die." The response brings a faint smile to Zorba's lips and, as he walks away, he exclaims with a note of irony: "How strange—I live as though I were going to die tomorrow!"

As a member of Alcoholics Anonymous, I have found that the Third Legacy is a fertile soil in which to plant the tree of my sobriety. The fruits I harvest are wonderful: peace, security, understanding and twenty-four hours of eternal fulfillment; and with the soundness of mind to listen to the voice of my conscience when, in silence, it gently speaks to me, saying: You must let go in service. There are others who must plant and harvest.

OUR GROUP CONSCIENCE

"*. . . sometimes the good is the enemy of the best.*"
ALCOHOLICS ANONYMOUS COMES OF AGE, p. 101

I think these words apply to every area of A.A.'s Three Legacies: Recovery, Unity and Service! I want them etched in my mind and life as I "trudge the Road of Happy Destiny" (*Alcoholics Anonymous, p. 164*). These words, often spoken by co-founder Bill W., were appropriately said to him as the result of the group's conscience. It brought home to Bill W. the essence of our Second Tradition: "Our leaders are but trusted servants; they do not govern."

Just as Bill W. was originally urged to remember, I think that in our group discussions we should never settle for the "good," but always strive to attain the "best." These common strivings are yet another example of a loving God, as we understand Him, expressing Himself through the group conscience. Experiences such as these help me to stay on the proper path of recovery. I learn to combine initiative with humility, responsibility with thankfulness, and thus relish the joys of living my twenty-four hour program.

NO ONE DENIED ME LOVE

*On the A.A. calendar it was Year Two. . . . A new-
comer appeared at one of these groups. . . . He
soon proved that his was a desperate case, and that
above all he wanted to get well. . . . [He said],
"Since I am the victim of another addiction even
worse stigmatized than alcoholism, you may not
want me among you."*
TWELVE STEPS AND TWELVE TRADITIONS, pp. 141–42

I came to you—a wife, mother, woman who had
walked out on her husband, children, family. I was
a drunk, a pill-head, a nothing. Yet no one denied
me love, caring, a sense of belonging. Today, by
God's grace and the love of a good sponsor and a
home group, I can say that—through you in Alcoholics Anonymous—I am a wife, a mother, a
grandmother and a woman. Sober. Free of pills. Responsible.

Without a Higher Power I found in the Fellowship, my life would be meaningless. I am full of
gratitude to be a member of good standing in Alcoholics Anonymous.

LOOKING WITHIN

Made a searching and fearless moral inventory of ourselves.

TWELVE STEPS AND TWELVE TRADITIONS, p. 42

Step Four is the vigorous and painstaking effort to discover what the liabilities in each of us have been, and are. I want to find exactly how, when, and where my natural desires have warped me. I wish to look squarely at the unhappiness this has caused others and myself. By discovering what my emotional deformities are, I can move toward their correction. Without a willing and persistent effort to do this, there can be little sobriety or contentment for me.

To resolve ambivalent feelings, I need to feel a strong and helpful sense of myself. Such an awareness doesn't happen overnight, and no one's self-awareness is permanent. Everyone has the capacity for growth, and for self-awareness, through an honest encounter with reality. When I don't avoid issues but meet them directly, always trying to resolve them, they become fewer and fewer.

CHARACTER BUILDING

Demands made upon other people for too much attention, protection, and love can only invite domination or revulsion. . . .
TWELVE STEPS AND TWELVE TRADITIONS, p. 44

When I uncovered my need for approval in the Fourth Step, I didn't think it should rank as a character defect. I wanted to think of it more as an asset (that is, the desire to please people). It was quickly pointed out to me that this "need" can be very crippling. Today I still enjoy getting the approval of others, but I am not willing to pay the price I used to pay to get it. I will not bend myself into a pretzel to get others to like me. If I get your approval, that's fine; but if I don't, I will survive without it. I am responsible for speaking what I perceive to be the truth, not what I think others may want to hear.

Similarly, my false pride always kept me overly concerned about my reputation. Since being enlightened in the A.A. program, my aim is to improve my character.

ACCEPTING OUR HUMANNESS

We finally saw that the inventory should be ours, not the other man's. So we admitted our wrongs honestly and became willing to set these matters straight.

AS BILL SEES IT, p. 222

Why is it that the alcoholic is so unwilling to accept responsibility? I used to drink because of the things that other people did to me. Once I came to A.A. I was told to look at where I had been wrong. What did I have to do with all these different matters? When I simply accepted that I had a part in them, I was able to put it on paper and see it for what it was —humanness. I am not expected to be perfect! I have made errors before and I will make them again. To be honest about them allows me to accept them—and myself—and those with whom I had the differences; from there, recovery is just a short distance ahead.

CRYING FOR THE MOON

"This very real feeling of inferiority is magnified by his childish sensitivity and it is this state of affairs which generates in him that insatiable, abnormal craving for self-approval and success in the eyes of the world. Still a child, he cries for the moon. And the moon, it seems, won't have him!"

LANGUAGE OF THE HEART, p. 102

While drinking I seemed to vacillate between feeling totally invisible and believing I was the center of the universe. Searching for that elusive balance between the two has become a major part of my recovery. The moon I constantly cried for is, in sobriety, rarely full; it shows me instead its many other phases, and there are lessons in them all. True learning has often followed an eclipse, a time of darkness, but with each cycle of my recovery, the light grows stronger and my vision is clearer.

TRUE BROTHERHOOD

We have not once sought to be one in a family, to be a friend among friends, to be a worker among workers, to be a useful member of society. Always we tried to struggle to the top of the heap, or to hide underneath it. This self-centered behavior blocked a partnership relation with any one of those about us. Of true brotherhood we had small comprehension.

TWELVE STEPS AND TWELVE TRADITIONS, p. 53

This message contained in Step Four was the first one I heard loud and clear; I hadn't seen myself in print before! Prior to my coming into A.A., I knew of no place that could teach me how to become a person among persons. From my very first meeting, I saw people doing just that and I wanted what they had. One of the reasons that I'm a happy, sober alcoholic today is that I'm learning this most important lesson.

A LIFETIME PROCESS

We were having trouble with personal relationships, we couldn't control our emotional natures, we were a prey to misery and depression, we couldn't make a living, we had a feeling of uselessness, we were full of fear, we were unhappy, we couldn't seem to be of real help to other people. . . .

ALCOHOLICS ANONYMOUS, p. 52

These words remind me that I have more problems than alcohol, that alcohol is only a symptom of a more pervasive disease. When I stopped drinking I began a lifetime process of recovery from unruly emotions, painful relationships, and unmanageable situations. This process is too much for most of us without help from a Higher Power and our friends in the Fellowship. When I began working the Steps of the A.A. program, many of these tangled threads unraveled but, little by little, the most broken places of my life straightened out. One day at a time, almost imperceptibly, I healed. Like a thermostat being turned down, my fears diminished. I began to experience moments of contentment. My emotions became less volatile. I am now once again a part of the human family.

A WIDE ARC OF GRATITUDE

And, speaking for Dr. Bob and myself, I gratefully declare that had it not been for our wives, Anne and Lois, neither of us could have lived to see A.A.'s beginning.

THE A.A. WAY OF LIFE, p. 67

Am I capable of such generous tribute and gratitude to *my* wife, parents and friends, without whose support I might never have survived to reach A.A.'s doors? I will work on this and try to see the plan my Higher Power is showing me which links our lives together.

AN INSIDE LOOK

We want to find exactly how, when, and where our natural desires have warped us. We wish to look squarely at the unhappiness this has caused others and ourselves. By discovering what our emotional deformities are, we can move toward their correction.
TWELVE STEPS AND TWELVE TRADITIONS, p. 43

Today I am no longer a slave to alcohol, yet in so many ways enslavement still threatens—my self, my desires, even my dreams. Yet without dreams I cannot exist; without dreams there is nothing to keep me moving forward.

I must look inside myself, to free myself. I must call upon God's power to face the person I've feared the most, the true me, the person God created me to be. Unless I can or until I do, I will always be running, and never be truly free. I ask God daily to show me such a freedom!

FREEDOM FROM "KING ALCOHOL"

. . . let us not suppose even for an instant that we are not under constraint. . . . Our former tyrant, King Alcohol, always stands ready again to clutch us to him. Therefore, freedom from alcohol is the great "must" that has to be achieved, else we go mad or die.

AS BILL SEES IT, p. 134

When drinking, I lived in spiritual, emotional, and sometimes, physical confinement. I had constructed my prison with bars of self-will and self-indulgence, from which I could not escape. Occasional dry spells that seemed to promise freedom would turn out to be little more than hopes of a reprieve. True escape required a willingness to follow whatever right actions were needed to turn the lock. With that willingness and action, both the lock and the bars themselves opened for me. Continued willingness and action keep me free—in a kind of extended daily probation—that need never end.

GROWING UP

The essence of all growth is a willingness to change for the better and then an unremitting willingness to shoulder whatever responsibility this entails.
AS BILL SEES IT, p. 115

Sometimes when I've become willing to do what I should have been doing all along, I want praise and recognition. I don't realize that the more I'm willing to act differently, the more exciting my life is. The more I am willing to help others, the more rewards I receive. That's what practicing the principles means to me. Fun and benefits for me are in the willingness to do the actions, not to get immediate results. Being a little kinder, a little slower to anger, a little more loving makes my life better—day by day.

A WORD TO DROP: "BLAME"

To see how erratic emotions victimized us often took a long time. We could perceive them quickly in others, but only slowly in ourselves. First of all, we had to admit that we had many of these defects, even though such disclosures were painful and humiliating. Where other people were concerned, we had to drop the word "blame" from our speech and thought.

TWELVE STEPS AND TWELVE TRADITIONS, p. 47

When I did my Fourth Step, following the Big Book guidelines, I noticed that my grudge list was filled with my prejudices and my blaming others for my not being able to succeed and to live up to my potential. I also discovered I felt different because I was black. As I continued to work on the Step, I learned that I always had drunk to rid myself of those feelings. It was only when I sobered up and worked on my inventory, that I could no longer blame anyone.

GIVING UP INSANITY

. . . where alcohol has been involved, we have been strangely insane.

ALCOHOLICS ANONYMOUS, p. 38

Alcoholism required me to drink, whether I wanted to or not. Insanity dominated my life and was the essence of my disease. It robbed me of the freedom of choice over drinking and, therefore, robbed me of all other choices. When I drank, I was unable to make effective choices in any part of my life and life became unmanageable.

I ask God to help me understand and accept the full meaning of the disease of alcoholism.

THE FALSE COMFORT OF SELF-PITY

Self-pity is one of the most unhappy and consuming defects that we know. It is a bar to all spiritual progress and can cut off all effective communication with our fellows because of its inordinate demands for attention and sympathy. It is a maudlin form of martyrdom, which we can ill afford.

AS BILL SEES IT, p. 238

The false comfort of self-pity screens me from reality only momentarily and then demands, like a drug, that I take an ever bigger dose. If I succumb to this it could lead to a relapse into drinking. What can I do? One certain antidote is to turn my attention, however slightly at first, toward others who are genuinely less fortunate than I, preferably other alcoholics. In the same degree that I actively demonstrate my empathy with them, I will lessen my own exaggerated suffering.

THE "NUMBER ONE OFFENDER"

Resentment is the "number one" offender. It destroys more alcoholics than anything else. From it stem all forms of spiritual disease, for we have been not only mentally and physically ill, we have been spiritually sick.

ALCOHOLICS ANONYMOUS, p. 64

As I look at myself practicing the Fourth Step, it is easy to gloss over the wrong that I have done, because I can easily see it as a question of "getting even" for a wrong done to me. If I continue to relive my old hurt, it is a resentment and resentment bars the sunlight from my soul. If I continue to relive hurts and hates, I will hurt and hate myself. After years in the dark of resentments, I have found the sunlight. I must let go of resentments; I cannot afford them.

THE BONDAGE OF RESENTMENTS

*. . . harboring resentment is infinitely grave. For
then we shut ourselves off from the sunlight of the
spirit.*

AS BILL SEES IT, p. 5

It has been said, "Anger is a luxury I cannot afford." Does this suggest I ignore this human emotion? I believe not. Before I learned of the A.A.
program, I was a slave to the behavior patterns of
alcoholism. I was chained to negativity, with no
hope of cutting loose.

The Steps offered me an alternative. Step Four
was the beginning of the end of my bondage. The
process of "letting go" started with an inventory. I
needed not be frightened, for the previous Steps as-
sured me I was not alone. My Higher Power led me
to this door and gave me the gift of choice. Today I
can choose to open the door to freedom and rejoice
in the sunlight of the Steps, as they cleanse the
spirit within me.

ANGER: A "DUBIOUS LUXURY"

If we were to live, we had to be free of anger. The grouch and the brainstorm were not for us. They may be the dubious luxury of the normal men, but for alcoholics these things are poison.

ALCOHOLICS ANONYMOUS, p. 66

"Dubious luxury." How often have I remembered those words. It's not just anger that's best left to nonalcoholics; I built a list including justifiable resentment, self-pity, judgmentalism, self-righteousness, false pride and false humility. I'm always surprised to read the actual quote. So well have the principles of the program been drummed into me that I keep thinking all of these defects are listed too. Thank God I can't afford them—or I surely would indulge in them.

LOVE AND FEAR AS OPPOSITES

All these failings generate fear, a soul-sickness in its own right.

TWELVE STEPS AND TWELVE TRADITIONS, p. 49

"Fear knocked at the door; faith answered; no one was there." I don't know to whom this quote should be attributed, but it certainly indicates very clearly that fear is an illusion. I create the illusion myself.

I experienced fear early in my life and I mistakenly thought that the mere presence of it made me a coward. I didn't know that one of the definitions of "courage" is "the willingness to do the right thing in spite of fear." Courage, then, is not necessarily the absence of fear.

During the times I didn't have love in my life I most assuredly had fear. To fear God is to be afraid of joy. In looking back, I realize that, during the times I feared God most, there was no joy in my life. As I learned not to fear God, I also learned to experience joy.

SELF-HONESTY

The deception of others is nearly always rooted in the deception of ourselves. . . . When we are honest with another person, it confirms that we have been honest with ourselves and with God.

AS BILL SEES IT, p. 17

When I was drinking, I deceived myself about reality, rewriting it to what I wanted it to be. Deceiving others is a character defect—even if it is just stretching the truth a bit or cleaning up my motives so others would think well of me. My Higher Power can remove this character defect, but first I have to help myself become willing to receive that help by not practicing deception. I need to remember each day that deceiving myself about myself is setting myself up for failure or disappointment in life and in Alcoholics Anonymous. A close, *honest* relationship with a Higher Power is the only solid foundation I've found for honesty with self and with others.

BROTHERS IN OUR DEFECTS

We recovered alcoholics are not so much brothers in virtue as we are brothers in our defects, and in our common strivings to overcome them.

AS BILL SEES IT, p. 167

The identification that one alcoholic has with another is mysterious, spiritual—almost incomprehensible. But it is there. I "feel" it. Today I feel that I can help people and that they can help me.

It is a new and exciting feeling for me to care for someone; to care what they are feeling, hoping for, praying for; to know their sadness, joy, horror, sorrow, grief; to want to share those feelings so that someone can have relief. I never knew how to do this—or how to try. I never even cared. The Fellowship of A.A., and God, are teaching me how to care about others.

SELF-EXAMINATION

. . . we ask God to direct our thinking, especially asking that it be divorced from self-pity, dishonest or self-seeking motives.

ALCOHOLICS ANONYMOUS, p. 86

When said sincerely, this prayer teaches me to be truly unselfish and humble, for even in doing good deeds I often used to seek approval and glory for myself. By examining my motives in all that I do, I can be of service to God and others, helping them do what they want to do. When I put God in charge of my thinking, much needless worry is eliminated and I believe He guides me throughout the day. When I eliminate thoughts of self-pity, dishonesty and self-centeredness as soon as they enter my mind, I find peace with God, my neighbor and myself.

CULTIVATING FAITH

"I don't think we can do anything very well in this world unless we practice it. And I don't believe we do A.A. too well unless we practice it. . . . We should practice . . . acquiring the spirit of service. We should attempt to acquire some faith, which isn't easily done, especially for the person who has always been very materialistic, following the standards of society today. But I think faith can be acquired; it can be acquired slowly; it has to be cultivated. That was not easy for me, and I assume that it is difficult for everyone else. . . ."

DR. BOB AND THE GOOD OLDTIMERS, pp. 307-08

Fear is often the force that prevents me from acquiring and cultivating the power of faith. Fear blocks my appreciation of beauty, tolerance, forgiveness, service, and serenity.

NEW SOIL . . . NEW ROOTS

Moments of perception can build into a lifetime of spiritual serenity, as I have excellent reason to know. Roots of reality, supplanting the neurotic under-brush, will hold fast despite the high winds of the forces which would destroy us, or which we would use to destroy ourselves.

AS BILL SEES IT, p. 173

I came to A.A. green—a seedling quivering with exposed taproots. It was for survival but it was a beginning. I stretched, developed, twisted, but with the help of others, my spirit eventually burst up from the roots. I was free. I acted, withered, went inside, prayed, acted again, understood anew, as one moment of perception struck. Up from my roots, spirit-arms lengthened into strong, green shoots: high-springing servants stepping skyward.

Here on earth God unconditionally continues the legacy of higher love. My A.A. life put me "on a different footing . . . [my] roots grasped a new soil" (*Alcoholics Anonymous*, p. 12).

A.A. IS NOT A CURE-ALL

It would be a product of false pride to claim that A.A. is a cure-all, even for alcoholism.

AS BILL SEES IT, p. 285

In my early years of sobriety I was full of pride, thinking that A.A. was the only source of treatment for a good and happy life. It certainly was the basic ingredient for my sobriety and even today, with over twelve years in the program, I am very involved in meetings, sponsorship and service. During the first four years of my recovery, I found it necessary to seek professional help, since my emotional health was extremely poor. There are those folks too, who have found sobriety and happiness in other organizations. A.A. taught me that I had a choice: to go to any lengths to enhance my sobriety. A.A. may not be a cure-all for everything, but it is the center of my sober living.

LEARNING TO LOVE OURSELVES

Alcoholism was a lonely business, even though we were surrounded by people who loved us. . . . We were trying to find emotional security either by dominating or by being dependent upon others. . . . We still vainly tried to be secure by some unhealthy sort of domination or dependence.

AS BILL SEES IT, p. 252

When I did my personal inventory I found that I had unhealthy relationships with most people in my life—my friends and family, for example. I always felt isolated and lonely. I drank to dull emotional pain.

It was through staying sober, having a good sponsor and working the Twelve Steps that I was able to build up my low self-esteem. First the Twelve Steps taught me to become my own best friend, and then, when I was able to love myself, I could reach out and love others.

ENTERING A NEW DIMENSION

In the late stages of our drinking, the will to resist has fled. Yet when we admit complete defeat and when we become entirely ready to try A.A. principles, our obsession leaves us and we enter a new dimension—freedom under God as we understand Him.

AS BILL SEES IT, p. 283

I am fortunate to be among the ones who have had this awesome transformation in my life. When I entered the doors of A.A., alone and desperate, I had been beaten into willingness to believe anything I heard. One of the things I heard was, "This *could* be your last hangover, or you can keep going round and round." The man who said this obviously was a whole lot better off than I. I liked the idea of admitting defeat and I have been free ever since! My heart heard what my mind never could: "Being powerless over alcohol is no big deal." I'm free and I'm grateful!

HAPPINESS IS NOT THE POINT

I don't think happiness or unhappiness is the point. How do we meet the problems we face? How do we best learn from them and transmit what we have learned to others, if they would receive the knowledge?

AS BILL SEES IT, p. 306

In my search "to be happy," I changed jobs, married and divorced, took geographical cures, and ran myself into debt—financially, emotionally and spiritually. In A.A., I'm learning to grow up. Instead of demanding that people, places and things make me happy, I can ask God for self-acceptance. When a problem overwhelms me, A.A.'s Twelve Steps will help me grow through the pain. The knowledge I gain can be a gift to others who suffer with the same problem. As Bill said, "When pain comes, we are expected to learn from it willingly, and help others to learn. When happiness comes, we accept it as a gift, and thank God for it." (*As Bill Sees It*, p. 306)

JOYFUL DISCOVERIES

We realize we know only a little. God will constantly disclose more to you and to us. Ask Him in your morning meditation what you can do each day for the man who is still sick. The answers will come, if your own house is in order. But obviously you cannot transmit something you haven't got. See to it that your relationship with Him is right, and great events will come to pass for you and countless others. This is the Great Fact for us.

ALCOHOLICS ANONYMOUS, p. 164

Sobriety is a journey of joyful discovery. Each day brings new experience, awareness, greater hope, deeper faith, broader tolerance. I must maintain these attributes or I will have nothing to pass on.

Great events for this recovering alcoholic are the normal everyday joys found in being able to live another day in God's grace.

TWO "MAGNIFICENT STANDARDS"

All A.A. progress can be reckoned in terms of just two words: humility and responsibility. Our whole spiritual development can be accurately measured by our degree of adherence to these magnificent standards.

AS BILL SEES IT, p. 271

To acknowledge and respect the views, accomplishments and prerogatives of others and to accept being wrong shows me the way of *humility*. To practice the principles of A.A. in all my affairs guides me to be *responsible*. Honoring these precepts gives credence to Tradition Four—and to all other Traditions of the Fellowship. Alcoholics Anonymous has evolved a philosophy of life full of valid motivations, rich in highly relevant principles and ethical values, a view of life which can be extended beyond the confines of the alcoholic population. To honor these precepts I need only to pray, and care for my fellow man as if each one were my brother.

GROUP AUTONOMY

Some may think that we have carried the principle of group autonomy to extremes. For example, in its original "long form," Tradition Four declares: "Any two or three gathered together for sobriety may call themselves an A.A. group, provided that as a group they have no other affiliation."* . . . But this ultra-liberty is not so risky as it looks.

A.A. COMES OF AGE, pp. 104-05

As an active alcoholic, I abused every liberty that life afforded. How could A.A. expect me to respect the "ultra-liberty" bestowed by Tradition Four? Learning respect has become a lifetime job.

A.A. has made me fully accept the necessity of discipline and that, if I do not assert it from within, then I will pay for it. This applies to groups too. Tradition Four points me in a spiritual direction, in spite of my alcoholic inclinations.

* This is a misquote; Bill quoted the Third Tradition, but was referring to Tradition Four.

A GREAT PARADOX

These legacies of suffering and of recovery are easily passed among alcoholics, one to the other. This is our gift from God, and its bestowal upon others like us is the one aim that today animates A.A.'s all around the globe.
TWELVE STEPS AND TWELVE TRADITIONS, p. 151

The great paradox of A.A. is that I know I cannot keep the precious gift of sobriety unless I give it away.

My primary purpose is to stay sober. In A.A. I have no other goal, and the importance of this is a matter of life or death for me. If I veer from this purpose I lose. But A.A. is not only for me; it is for the alcoholic who still suffers. The legions of recovering alcoholics stay sober by sharing with fellow alcoholics. The way to my recovery is to show others in A.A. that when I share with them, we both grow in the grace of the Higher Power, and both of us are on the road to a happy destiny.

HEALING HEART AND MIND

Admitted to God, to ourselves, and to another human being the exact nature of our wrongs.
TWELVE STEPS AND TWELVE TRADITIONS, p. 55

Since it is true that God comes to me through people, I can see that by keeping people at a distance I also keep God at a distance. God is nearer to me than I think and I can experience Him by loving people and allowing people to love me. But I can neither love nor be loved if I allow my secrets to get in the way.

It's the side of myself that I refuse to look at that rules me. I must be willing to look at the dark side in order to heal my mind and heart because that is the road to freedom. I must walk into darkness to find the light and walk into fear to find peace.

By revealing my secrets—and thereby ridding myself of guilt—I can actually change my thinking; by altering my thinking, I can change myself. My thoughts create my future. What I will be tomorrow is determined by what I think today.

LIGHTING THE DARK PAST

Cling to the thought that, in God's hands, the dark past is the greatest possession you have—the key to life and happiness for others. With it you can avert death and misery for them.

ALCOHOLICS ANONYMOUS, p. 124

No longer is my past an autobiography; it is a reference book to be taken down, opened and shared. Today as I report for duty, the most wonderful picture comes through. For, though this day be dark—as some days must be—the stars will shine even brighter later. My witness that they do shine will be called for in the very near future. All my past will this day be a part of me, because it is the key, not the lock.

CLEANING HOUSE

Somehow, being alone with God doesn't seem as embarrassing as facing up to another person. Until we actually sit down and talk aloud about what we have so long hidden, our willingness to clean house is still largely theoretical.

TWELVE STEPS AND TWELVE TRADITIONS, p. 60

It wasn't unusual for me to talk to God, and myself, about my character defects. But to sit down, face to face, and openly discuss these intimacies with another person was much more difficult. I recognized in the experience, however, a similar relief to the one I had experienced when I first admitted I was an alcoholic. I began to appreciate the spiritual significance of the program and that this Step was just an introduction to what was yet to come in the remaining seven Steps.

"ENTIRELY HONEST"

*We must be entirely honest with somebody if we ex-
pect to live long or happily in this world.*
ALCOHOLICS ANONYMOUS, p. 73-74

Honesty, like all virtues, is to be shared. It began
after I shared ". . . [my] whole life's story with
someone . . . " in order to find my place in the
Fellowship. Later I shared my life in order to help
the newcomer find his place with us. This sharing
helps me to learn honesty in all my dealings and to
know that God's plan for me comes true through
honest openness and willingness.

THE FOREST *AND* THE TREES

. . . what comes to us alone may be garbled by our own rationalization and wishful thinking. The benefit of talking to another person is that we can get his direct comment and counsel on our situation. . . .
TWELVE STEPS AND TWELVE TRADITIONS, p. 60

I cannot count the times when I have been angry and frustrated and said to myself, "I can't see the forest for the trees!" I finally realized that what I needed when I was in such pain was someone who could guide me in separating the forest and the trees; who could suggest a better path to follow; who could assist me in putting out fires; and help me avoid the rocks and pitfalls.

I ask God, when I'm in the forest, to give me the courage to call upon a member of A.A.

"HOLD BACK NOTHING"

The real tests of the situation are your own willing-ness to confide and your full confidence in the one with whom you share your first accurate self-survey. . . . Provided you hold back nothing, your sense of relief will mount from minute to minute. The dammed-up emotions of years break out of their confinement, and miraculously vanish as soon as they are exposed. As the pain subsides, a healing tranquility takes its place.
TWELVE STEPS AND TWELVE TRADITIONS, p. 61-62

A tiny kernel of locked-in feelings began to unfold when I first attended A.A. meetings and self-knowledge then became a learning task for me. This new self-understanding brought about a change in my responses to life's situations. I realized I had the right to make choices in my life, and the inner dictatorship of habits slowly lost its grip.

I believe that if I seek God I can find a better way to live and I ask Him daily to assist me in living a sober life.

RESPECT FOR OTHERS

Such parts of our story we tell to someone who will understand, yet be unaffected. The rule is we must be hard on ourself, but always considerate of others.
ALCOHOLICS ANONYMOUS, p. 74

Respect for others is the lesson that I take out of this passage. I must go to any lengths to free myself if I wish to find that peace of mind that I have sought for so long. However, none of this must be done at another's expense. Selfishness has no place in the A.A. way of life.

When I take the Fifth Step it's wiser to choose a person with whom I share common aims because if that person does not understand me, my spiritual progress may be delayed and I could be in danger of a relapse. So I ask for divine guidance before choosing the man or woman whom I take into my confidence.

A RESTING PLACE

All of A.A.'s Twelve Steps ask us to go contrary to our natural desires . . . they all deflate our egos. When it comes to ego deflation, few Steps are harder to take than Five. But scarcely any Step is more necessary to longtime sobriety and peace of mind than this one.

TWELVE STEPS AND TWELVE TRADITIONS, p. 55

After writing down my character defects, I was unwilling to talk about them, and decided it was time to stop carrying this burden alone. I needed to confess those defects to someone else. I had read—and been told—I could not stay sober unless I did. Step Five provided me with a feeling of belonging, with humility and serenity when I practiced it in my daily living. It was important to admit my defects of character in the order presented in Step Five: "to God, to ourselves and to another human being." Admitting to God first paved the way for admission to myself and to another person. As the taking of the Step is described, a feeling of being at one with God and my fellow man brought me to a resting place where I could prepare myself for the remaining Steps toward a full and meaningful sobriety.

WALKING THROUGH FEAR

If we still cling to something we will not let go, we ask God to help us be willing.

ALCOHOLICS ANONYMOUS, p. 76

When I had taken my Fifth Step, I became aware that all my defects of character stemmed from my need to feel secure and loved. To use *my* will alone to work on them would have been trying obsessively to solve the problem. In the Sixth Step I intensified the action I had taken in the first three Steps—meditating on the Step by saying it over and over, going to meetings, following my sponsor's suggestions, reading and searching within myself. During the first three years of sobriety I had a fear of entering an elevator alone. One day I decided I must walk through this fear. I asked for God's help, entered the elevator, and there in the corner was a lady crying. She said that since her husband had died she was deathly afraid of elevators. I forgot my fear and comforted her. This spiritual experience helped me to see how willingness was the key to working the rest of the Twelve Steps to recovery. God helps those who help themselves.

FREE AT LAST

Another great dividend we may expect from confiding our defects to another human being is humility —a word often misunderstood. . . . it amounts to a clear recognition of what and who we really are, followed by a sincere attempt to become what we could be.

TWELVE STEPS AND TWELVE TRADITIONS, p. 58

I knew deep inside that if I were ever to be joyous, happy and free, I had to share my past life with some other individual. The joy and relief I experienced after doing so were beyond description. Almost immediately after taking the Fifth Step, I felt free from the bondage of self and the bondage of alcohol. That freedom remains after 36 years, a day at a time. I found that God could do for me what I couldn't do for myself.

A NEW SENSE OF BELONGING

Until we had talked with complete candor of our conflicts, and had listened to someone else do the same thing, we still didn't belong.
TWELVE STEPS AND TWELVE TRADITIONS, p. 57

After four years in A.A. I was able to discover the freedom from the burden of buried emotions that had caused me so much pain. With the help of A.A., and extra counseling, the pain was released and I felt a complete sense of belonging and peace. I also felt a joy and a love of God that I had never experienced before. I am in awe of the power of Step Five.

THE PAST IS OVER

A.A. experience has taught us we cannot live alone with our pressing problems and the character defects which cause or aggravate them. If . . . Step Four . . . has revealed in stark relief those experiences we'd rather not remember . . . then the need to quit living by ourselves with those tormenting ghosts of yesterday gets more urgent than ever. We have to talk to somebody about them.

TWELVE STEPS AND TWELVE TRADITIONS, p. 55

Whatever is done is over. It cannot be changed. But my attitude about it can be changed through talking with those who have gone before and with sponsors. I can wish the past never was, but if I change my actions in regard to what I have done, my attitude will change. I won't have to wish the past away. I can change my feelings and attitudes, but only through my actions and the help of my fellow alcoholics.

THE EASIER, SOFTER WAY

If we skip this vital step, we may not overcome drinking.

ALCOHOLICS ANONYMOUS, p. 72

I certainly didn't leap at the opportunity to face who I was, especially when the pains of my drinking days hung over me like a dark cloud. But I soon heard at the meetings about the fellow member who just didn't want to take Step Five and kept coming back to meetings, trembling from the horrors of reliving his past. *The easier, softer way* is to take these Steps to freedom from our fatal disease, and to put our faith in the Fellowship and our Higher Power.

IT'S OKAY TO BE ME

Time after time newcomers have tried to keep to themselves certain facts about their lives. . . . they have turned to easier methods. . . . But they had not learned enough humility. . . .

ALCOHOLICS ANONYMOUS, pp. 72-73

Humility sounds so much like humiliation, but it really is the ability to look at myself—and honestly accept what I find. I no longer need to be the "smartest" or "dumbest" or any other "est." Finally, it is okay to be me. It is easier for me to accept myself if I share my whole life. If I cannot share in meetings, then I had better have a sponsor —someone with whom I can share those "certain facts" that could lead me back to a drunk, to death. I need to take all the Steps. I need the Fifth Step to learn true humility. Easier methods do not work.

KNOW GOD; KNOW PEACE

It is plain that a life which includes deep resentment leads only to futility and unhappiness. . . . But with the alcoholic, whose hope is the maintenance and growth of a spiritual experience, this business of resentment is infinitely grave.

ALCOHOLICS ANONYMOUS, p. 66

Know God;
Know peace.
No God;
No peace.

WE FORGIVE . . .

Often it was while working on this Step with our sponsors or spiritual advisers that we first felt truly able to forgive others, no matter how deeply we felt they had wronged us. Our moral inventory had persuaded us that all-round forgiveness was desirable, but it was only when we resolutely tackled Step Five that we inwardly knew we'd be able to receive forgiveness and give it, too.

TWELVE STEPS AND TWELVE TRADITIONS, p. 58

What a great feeling forgiveness is! What a revelation about my emotional, psychological and spiritual nature. All it takes is willingness to forgive; God will do the rest.

. . . AND FORGIVE

Under very trying conditions I have had, again and again, to forgive others—also myself.

AS BILL SEES IT, p. 268

Forgiveness of self and forgiveness of others are just two currents in the same river, both hindered or shut off completely by the dam of resentment. Once that dam is lifted, both currents can flow. The Steps of A.A. allow me to see how resentment has built up and subsequently blocked off this flow in my life. The Steps provide a way by which my resentments may—by the grace of God as I understand Him— be lifted. It is as a result of this solution that I can find the necessary grace which enables me to forgive myself and others.

FREEDOM TO BE ME

If we are painstaking about this phase of our development, we will be amazed before we are half way through. We are going to know a new freedom and a new happiness.

ALCOHOLICS ANONYMOUS, p. 83

My first true freedom is the freedom not to have to take a drink today. If I truly want it, I will work the Twelve Steps and the happiness of this freedom will come to me through the Steps—sometimes quickly, sometimes slowly. Other freedoms will follow, and inventorying them is a new happiness. I had a new freedom today, the freedom to be me. I have the freedom to be the best me I have ever been.

GIVING WITHOUT STRINGS

And he well knows that his own life has been made richer, as an extra dividend of giving to another without any demand for a return.

AS BILL SEES IT, p. 69

The concept of giving without strings was hard to understand when I first came into the program. I was suspicious when others wanted to help me. I thought, "What do they want in return?" But I soon learned the joy of helping another alcoholic and I understood why they were there for me in the beginning. My attitudes changed and I wanted to help others. Sometimes I became anxious, as I wanted them to know the joys of sobriety, that life can be beautiful. When my life is full of a loving God of my understanding and I give that love to my fellow alcoholic, I feel a special richness that is hard to explain.

ONE DAY AT A TIME

Above all, take it one day at a time.

AS BILL SEES IT, p. 11

Why do I kid myself that I must stay away from a drink for only one day, when I know perfectly well I must never drink again as long as I live? I am not kidding myself because one day at a time is probably the only way I can reach the long-range objective of staying sober.

If I determine that I shall never drink again as long as I live, I set myself up. How can I be sure I won't drink when I have no idea what the future may hold?

On a day-at-a-time basis, I am confident I can stay away from a drink for one day. So I set out with confidence. At the end of the day, I have the reward of achievement. Achievement feels good and that makes me want more!

A LIST OF BLESSINGS

One exercise that I practice is to try for a full inventory of my blessings. . . .

AS BILL SEES IT, p. 37

What did I have to be grateful for? I shut myself up and started listing the blessings for which I was in no way responsible, beginning with having been born of sound mind and body. I went through seventy-four years of living right up to the present moment. The list ran to two pages, and took two hours to compile; I included health, family, money, A.A. —the whole gamut.

Every day in my prayers, I ask God to help me remember my list, and to be grateful for it throughout the day. When I remember my gratitude list, it's very hard to conclude that God is picking on me.

STEP ONE

WE . . . (The first word of the First Step)
TWELVE STEPS AND TWELVE TRADITIONS, p. 21

When I was drinking all I could ever think about was "I, I, I," or "Me, Me, Me." Such painful obsession of self, such soul sickness, such spiritual selfishness bound me to the bottle for more than half my life.

The journey to find God and to do His will one day at a time began with the first word of the First Step . . . "We." There was power in numbers, there was strength in numbers, there was safety in numbers, and for an alcoholic like me, there was life in numbers. If I had tried to recover alone I probably would have died. With God and another alcoholic I have a divine purpose in my life . . . I have become a channel for God's healing love.

SPIRITUAL HEALTH

When the spiritual malady is overcome, we straighten out mentally and physically.
ALCOHOLICS ANONYMOUS, p. 64

It is very difficult for me to come to terms with my spiritual illness because of my great pride, disguised by my material successes and my intellectual power. Intelligence is not incompatible with humility, provided I place humility first. To seek prestige and wealth is the ultimate goal for many in the modern world. To be fashionable and to seem better than I really am is a spiritual illness.

To recognize and to admit my weaknesses is the beginning of good spiritual health. It is a sign of spiritual health to be able to ask God every day to enlighten me, to recognize His will, and to have the strength to execute it. My spiritual health is excellent when I realize that the better I get, the more I discover how much help I need from others.

"HAPPY, JOYOUS AND FREE"

We are sure God wants us to be happy, joyous, and free. We cannot subscribe to the belief that this life is a vale of tears, though it once was just that for many of us. But it is clear that we made our own misery. God didn't do it. Avoid then, the deliberate manufacture of misery, but if trouble comes, cheerfully capitalize it as an opportunity to demonstrate His omnipotence.

ALCOHOLICS ANONYMOUS, p. 133

For years I believed in a punishing God and blamed Him for my misery. I have learned that I must lay down the "weapons" of self in order to pick up the "tools" of the A.A. program. I do not struggle with the program because it is a gift and I have never struggled when receiving a gift. If I sometimes keep on struggling, it is because I'm still hanging onto my old ideas and " . . . the results are nil."

PROGRESSIVE GRATITUDE

Gratitude should go forward, rather than backward.
AS BILL SEES IT, p 29

I am very grateful that my Higher Power has given me a second chance to live a worthwhile life. Through Alcoholics Anonymous, I have been restored to sanity. The promises are being fulfilled in my life. I am grateful to be free from the slavery of alcohol. I am grateful for peace of mind and the opportunity to grow, but my gratitude should go forward rather than backward. I cannot stay sober on yesterday's meetings or past Twelfth-Step calls; I need to put my gratitude into action *today*. Our co-founder said our gratitude can best be shown by carrying the message to others. Without action, my gratitude is just a pleasant emotion. I need to put it into action by working Step Twelve, by carrying the message and practicing the principles in all my affairs. I am grateful for the chance to carry the message today!

TURNING NEGATIVE TO POSITIVE

Our spiritual and emotional growth in A.A. does not depend so deeply upon success as it does upon our failures and setbacks. If you will bear this in mind, I think that your slip will have the effect of kicking you upstairs, instead of down.

AS BILL SEES IT, p. 184

In keeping with the pain and adversity which our founders encountered and overcame in establishing A.A., Bill W. sent us a clear message: a relapse can provide a positive experience toward abstinence and a lifetime of recovery. A relapse brings truth to what we hear repeatedly in meetings—"Don't take that first drink!" It reinforces the belief in the progressive nature of the disease, and it drives home the need for, and beauty of, humility in our spiritual program. Simple truths come in complicated ways to me when I become ego driven.

NO MAUDLIN GUILT

Day by day, we try to move a little toward God's perfection. So we need not be consumed by maudlin guilt. . . .

AS BILL SEES IT, p. 15

When I first discovered that there is not a single "don't" in the Twelve Steps of A.A., I was disturbed because this discovery swung open a giant portal. Only then was I able to realize what A.A. is for me:

A.A. is not a program of "don't"s, but of "do's."
A.A. is not martial law; it is freedom.
A.A. is not tears over defects, but sweat over
fixing them.
A.A. is not penitence; it is salvation.
A.A. is not "Woe to me" for my sins, past
and present.
A.A. is "Praise God" for the progress I am
making today.

EQUAL RIGHTS

At one time or another most A.A. groups go on rule-making benders. . . . After a time fear and intolerance subside. [and we realize] We do not wish to deny anyone his chance to recover from alcoholism. We wish to be just as inclusive as we can, never exclusive.

"A.A. TRADITION: HOW IT DEVELOPED," pp. 10, 11, 12

A.A. offered me complete freedom and accepted me into the Fellowship for myself. Membership did not depend upon conformity, financial success or education and I am so grateful for that. I often ask myself if I extend the same equality to others or if I deny them the freedom to be different. Today I try to replace my fear and intolerance with faith, patience, love and acceptance. I can bring these strengths to my A.A. group, my home and my office. I make an effort to bring my positive attitude everywhere that I go.

I have neither the right, nor the responsibility, to judge others. Depending on my attitude I can view newcomers to A.A., family members and friends as menaces or as teachers. When I think of some of my past judgments, it is clear how my self-righteousness caused me spiritual harm.

TRUE TOLERANCE

The only requirement for A.A. membership is a desire to stop drinking.
TWELVE STEPS AND TWELVE TRADITIONS, p. 139

I first heard the short form of the Third Tradition in the Preamble. When I came to A.A. I could not accept myself, my alcoholism, or a Higher Power. If there had been any physical, mental, moral, or religious requirements for membership, I would be dead today. Bill W. said in his tape on the Traditions that the Third Tradition is a charter for individual freedom. The most impressive thing to me was the feeling of acceptance from members who were practicing the Third Tradition by tolerating and accepting me. I feel acceptance is love and love is God's will for us.

OUR PRIMARY PURPOSE

The more A.A. sticks to its primary purpose, the greater will be its helpful influence everywhere.
A.A. COMES OF AGE, p. 109

It is with gratitude that I reflect on the early days of our Fellowship and those wise and loving "foresteppers" who proclaimed that we should not be diverted from our primary purpose, that of carrying the message to the alcoholic who still suffers.

I desire to impart respect to those who labor in the field of alcoholism, being ever mindful that A.A. endorses no causes other than its own. I must remember that A.A. has no monopoly on miracle-making and I remain humbly grateful to a loving God who made A.A. possible.

READINESS TO SERVE OTHERS

. . . our Society has concluded that it has but one high mission—to carry the A.A. message to those who don't know there's a way out.
TWELVE STEPS AND TWELVE TRADITIONS, p. 151

The "Light" to freedom shines bright on my fellow alcoholics as each one of us challenges the other to grow. The "Steps" to self-improvement have small beginnings, but each Step builds the "ladder" out of the pit of despair to new hope. Honesty becomes my "tool" to unfurl the "chains" which bound me. A sponsor, who is a caring listener, can help me to truly hear the message guiding me to freedom.

I ask God for the courage to live in such a way that the Fellowship may be a testimony to His favor. This mission frees me to share my gifts of wellness through a spirit of readiness to serve others.

A CHANGED OUTLOOK

Our whole attitude and outlook upon life will change.

ALCOHOLICS ANONYMOUS, p. 84

When I was drinking, my attitude was totally self-ish, totally self-centered; my pleasure and my comfort came first. Now that I am sober, self-seeking has started to slip away. My whole attitude toward life and other people is changing. For me, the first "A" in our name stands for *attitude*. My attitude is changed by the second "A" in our name, which stands for *action*. By working the Steps, attending meetings, and carrying the message, I can be restored to sanity. Action is the magic word! With a positive, helpful attitude and regular A.A. action, I can stay sober and help others to achieve sobriety. My attitude now is that I am willing to go to any length to stay sober!

THE UPWARD PATH

Here are the steps we took. . . .
ALCOHOLICS ANONYMOUS, p. 59

These are the words that lead into the Twelve Steps. In their direct simplicity they sweep aside all psychological and philosophical considerations about the rightness of the Steps. They describe what I did: I took the Steps and sobriety was the result. These words do not imply that I should walk the well-trodden path of those who went before, but rather that there is a way for me to become sober and that it is a way I shall have to find. It is a new path, one that leads to infinite light at the top of the mountain. The Steps advise me about the footholds that are safe and about chasms to avoid. They provide me with the tools I need during the many parts of the solitary journey of my soul. When I speak of this journey, I share my experience, strength and hope with others.

ON A WING AND A PRAYER

. . . we then look at Step Six. *We have emphasized willingness as being indispensable.*

ALCOHOLICS ANONYMOUS, p. 76

Steps Four and Five were difficult, but worthwhile. Now I was stuck on Step Six and, in despair, I picked up the Big Book and read this passage. I was outside, praying for willingness, when I raised my eyes and saw a huge bird rising in the sky. I watched it suddenly give itself up to the powerful air currents of the mountains. Swept along, swooping and soaring, the bird did things seemingly impossible for mortal birds to do. It was an inspiring example of a fellow creature "letting go" to a power greater than itself. I realized that if the bird "took back his will" and tried to fly with less trust, on its power alone, it would spoil its apparent free flight. That insight granted me the willingness to pray the Seventh Step prayer.

It's not easy to know God's will in each circumstance. I must search out and be ready for the currents, and that's where prayer and meditation help! Because I am, of myself, nothing, I ask God to grant me the knowledge of His will and the power and courage to carry it out—today.

LETTING GO OF OUR OLD SELVES

Carefully reading the first five proposals we ask if we have omitted anything, for we are building an arch through which we shall walk a free man at last. . . . Are we now ready to let God remove from us all the things which we have admitted are objectionable?

ALCOHOLICS ANONYMOUS, pp. 75, 76

The Sixth Step is the last "preparation" Step. Although I have already used prayer extensively, I have made no formal request of my Higher Power in the first Six Steps. I have identified my problem, come to believe that there is a solution, made a decision to seek this solution, and have "cleaned house." I now ask: Am I willing to live a life of sobriety, of change, to let go of my old self? I must determine if I am truly ready to change. I review what I have done and become willing for God to remove all my defects of character; for in the next Step, I will tell my Creator I am willing and will ask for help. If I have been thorough in the preparation of my foundation and feel that I am willing to change, I am then ready to continue with the next Step. "If we still cling to something we will not let go, we ask God to help us be willing." (*Alcoholics Anonymous*, p. 76)

ENTIRELY READY?

"This is the Step that separates the men from the boys.". . . *the difference between "the boys and the men" is the difference between striving for a self-determined objective and for the perfect objective which is of God.* . . . *It is suggested that we ought to become entirely willing to aim toward perfection.* . . . *The moment we say, "No, never!" our minds close against the grace of God.* . . . *This is the exact point at which we abandon limited objectives, and move toward God's will for us.*
TWELVE STEPS AND TWELVE TRADITIONS, pp. 63, 68, 69

Am I entirely ready to have God remove these defects of character? Do I know at long last that I cannot save myself? I have come to believe that I cannot. If I am unable, if my best intentions go wrong, if my desires are selfishly motivated and if my knowledge and will are limited—then I am ready to embrace God's will for my life.

ALL WE DO IS TRY

Can He now take them all—every one?
ALCOHOLICS ANONYMOUS, p. 76

In doing Step Six it helped me a lot to remember that I am striving for "spiritual progress." Some of my character defects may be with me for the rest of my life, but most have been toned down or eliminated. All that Step Six asks of me is to become willing to name my defects, claim them as my own, and be willing to discard the ones I can, just for today. As I grow in the program, many of my defects become more objectionable to me than previously and, therefore, I need to repeat Step Six so that I can become happier with myself and maintain my serenity.

LONG-TERM HOPE

Since most of us are born with an abundance of natural desires, it isn't strange that we often let these far exceed their intended purpose. When they drive us blindly, or we willfully demand that they supply us with more satisfactions or pleasures than are possible or due us, that is the point at which we depart from the degree of perfection that God wishes for us here on earth. That is the measure of our character defects, or, if you wish, of our sins.
TWELVE STEPS AND TWELVE TRADITIONS, p. 65

This is where long-term hope is born and perspective is gained, both of the nature of my illness and the path of my recovery. The beauty of A.A. lies in knowing that my life, with God's help, will improve. The A.A. journey becomes richer, the understanding becomes truth, the dreams become realities—and today becomes forever.

As I step into the A.A. light, my heart fills with the presence of God.

OPENING UP TO CHANGE

Self-searching is the means by which we bring new vision, action, and grace to bear upon the dark and negative side of our natures. With it comes the development of that kind of humility that makes it possible for us to receive God's help. . . . we find that bit by bit we can discard the old life—the one that did not work—for a new life that can and does work under any conditions whatever.

AS BILL SEES IT, pp. 10, 8

I have been given a daily reprieve contingent upon my spiritual condition, provided I seek progress, not perfection. To become ready for change, I practice willingness, opening myself to possibilities of change. If I realize there are defects that hinder my usefulness in A.A. and toward others, I become ready by meditating and receiving direction. "Some of us have tried to hold on to our old ideas and the result was nil until we let go absolutely" (*Alcoholics Anonymous,* p. 58). To let go and let God, I need only surrender my old ways to Him; I no longer fight nor do I try to control, but simply believe that, with God's help, I am changed and affirming this belief makes me ready. I empty myself to be full of awareness, light, and love, and I am ready to face each day with hope.

LIVING IN THE NOW

First, we try living in the now just in order to stay sober—and it works. Once the idea has become a part of our thinking, we find that living life in 24-hour segments is an effective and satisfying way to handle many other matters as well.

LIVING SOBER, p. 7

"One Day At A Time." To a newcomer this and other one-liners of A.A. may seem ridiculous. The passwords of the A.A. Fellowship can become life-lines in moments of stress. Each day can be like a rose unfurling according to the plan of a Power greater than myself. My program should be planted in the right location, just as it will need to be groomed, nourished, and protected from disease. My planting will require patience, and my realizing that some flowers will be more perfect than others. Each stage of the petals' unfolding can bring wonder and delight if I do not interfere or let my expectations override my acceptance—and this brings serenity.

IMPATIENT? TRY LEVITATING

We reacted more strongly to frustrations than normal people.

AS BILL SEES IT, p. 111

Impatience with other people is one of my principal failings. Following a slow car in a no-passing lane, or waiting in a restaurant for the check, drives me to distraction. Before I give God a chance to slow me down, I explode, and that's what I call being quicker than God. That repeated experience gave me an idea. I thought if I could look down on these events from God's point of view, I might better control my feelings and behavior. I tried it and when I encountered the next slow driver, I levitated and looked down on the other car and upon myself. I saw an elderly couple driving along, happily chatting about their grandchildren. They were followed by me—bug-eyed and red of face—who had no time schedule to meet anyway. I looked so silly that I dropped back into reality and slowed down. Seeing things from God's angle of vision can be very relaxing.

FAMILY OBLIGATIONS

*. . . a spiritual life which does not in-
clude . . . family obligations may not be so perfect
after all.*

ALCOHOLICS ANONYMOUS, p. 129

I can be doing great in the program—applying it at
meetings, at work, and in service activities—and
find that things have gone to pieces at home. I expect my loved ones to understand, but they cannot.
I expect them to see and value my progress, but
they don't—unless I *show* them. Do I neglect their
needs and desires for my attention and concern?
When I'm around them, am I irritable or boring?
Are my "amends" a mumbled "Sorry," or do they
take the form of patience and tolerance? Do I
preach to them, trying to reform or "fix" them?
Have I ever really cleaned house with *them*? "The
spiritual life is not a theory. *We have to live it*"
(*Alcoholics Anonymous*, p. 83).

FORMING TRUE PARTNERSHIPS

But it is from our twisted relations with family, friends, and society at large that many of us have suffered the most. We have been especially stupid and stubborn about them. The primary fact that we fail to recognize is our total inability to form a true partnership with another human being.

TWELVE STEPS AND TWELVE TRADITIONS, p. 53

Can these words apply to me, am I *still* unable to form a true partnership with another human being? What a terrible handicap that would be for me to carry into my sober life! In my sobriety I will meditate and pray to discover how I may be a trusted friend and companion.

LIVING OUR AMENDS

"Years of living with an alcoholic is almost sure to make any wife or child neurotic. The entire family is, to some extent, ill."

ALCOHOLICS ANONYMOUS, p. 122

It is important for me to realize that, as an alcoholic, I not only hurt myself, but also those around me. Making amends to my family, and to the families of alcoholics still suffering, will always be important. Understanding the havoc I created and trying to repair the destruction, will be a lifelong endeavor. The example of my sobriety may give others hope, and faith to help themselves.

WHEN THE GOING GETS ROUGH.

It is a design for living that works in rough going.
ALCOHOLICS ANONYMOUS, p. 15

When I came to A.A., I realized that A.A. worked wonderfully to help keep me sober. But could it work on real life problems, not concerned with drinking? I had my doubts. After being sober for more than two years I got my answer. I lost my job, developed physical problems, my diabetic father lost a leg, and someone I loved left me for another —and all of this happened during a two-week period. Reality crashed in, yet A.A. was there to support, comfort, and strengthen me. The principles I had learned during my early days of sobriety became a mainstay of my life for not only did I come through, but I never stopped being able to help newcomers. A.A. taught me not to be overwhelmed, but rather to accept and understand my life as it unfolded.

MAKING A.A. YOUR HIGHER POWER

". . .You can . . . make A.A. itself your 'higher power.' Here's a very large group of people who have solved their alcohol problem. . . . many members . . . have crossed the threshold just this way. . . . their faith broadened and deepened. . . . transformed, they came to believe in a Higher Power. . . ."
TWELVE STEPS AND TWELVE TRADITIONS, pp. 27-28

No one was greater than I, at least in my eyes, when I was drinking. Nevertheless, I couldn't smile at myself in the mirror, so I came to A.A. where, with others, I heard talk of a Higher Power. I couldn't accept the concept of a Higher Power because I believed God was cruel and unloving. In desperation I chose a table, a tree, then my A.A. group, as my Higher Power. Time passed, my life improved, and I began to wonder about this Higher Power. Gradually, with patience, humility and a lot of questions, I came to believe in God. Now my relationship with my Higher Power gives me the strength to live a happy, sober life.

OPEN-MINDEDNESS

We have found that God does not make too hard terms with those who seek Him. To us, the realm of spirit is broad, roomy, all inclusive, never exclusive or forbidding to those who earnestly seek. It is open, we believe, to all men.

AS BILL SEES IT, p. 7

Open-mindedness to concepts of a Higher Power can open doors to the spirit. Often I find the human spirit in various dogmas and faiths. I can be spiritual in the sharing of myself. The sharing of self joins me to the human race and brings me closer to God, as I understand Him.

"DEEP DOWN WITHIN US"

We found the Great Reality deep down within us. In the last analysis it is only there that He may be found. . . . search diligently within yourself. . . . With this attitude you cannot fail. The consciousness of your belief is sure to come to you.
ALCOHOLICS ANONYMOUS, p. 55

It was out of the depths of loneliness, depression and despair that I sought the help of A.A. As I recovered and began to face the emptiness and ruin of my life, I began to open myself to the possibility of the healing that recovery offers through the A.A. program. By coming to meetings, staying sober, and taking the Steps, I had the opportunity to listen with increasing attentiveness to the depths of my soul. Daily I waited, in hope and gratitude, for that sure belief and steadfast love I had longed for in my life. In this process, I met my God, as I understand Him.

A FELLOWSHIP OF FREEDOM

. . . if only men were granted absolute liberty, and were compelled to obey no one, they would then voluntarily associate themselves in the common interest.
AS BILL SEES IT, p. 50

When I no longer live under the dictates of another or of alcohol, I live in a new freedom. When I release the past and all the excess baggage I have carried for so very long, I come to know freedom. I have been introduced into a life and a fellowship of freedom. The Steps are a "recommended" way of finding a new life, there are no commands or dictates in A.A. I am free to serve from desire rather than decree. There is the understanding that I will benefit from the growth of other members and I take what I learn and bring it back to the group. The "common welfare" finds room to grow in the society of personal freedom.

"A.A. REGENERATION"

Such is the paradox of A.A. regeneration: strength arising out of complete defeat and weakness, the loss of one's old life as a condition for finding a new one.
A.A. COMES OF AGE, p. 46

A thousand beatings by John Barleycorn did not encourage me to admit defeat. I believed it was my moral obligation to conquer my "enemy-friend." At my first A.A. meeting I was blessed with a *feeling* that it was all right to admit defeat to a disease which had nothing to do with my "moral fiber." I knew instinctively that I was in the presence of a great love when I entered the doors of A.A. With no effort on my part, I became aware that to love myself was good and right, as God had intended. My feelings set me free, where my thoughts had held me in bondage. I am grateful.

RELEASE FROM FEAR

The problem of resolving fear has two aspects. We shall have to try for all the freedom from fear that is possible for us to attain. Then we shall need to find both the courage and grace to deal constructively with whatever fears remain.

AS BILL SEES IT, p. 61

Most of my decisions were based on fear. Alcohol made life easier to face, but the time came when alcohol was no longer an alternative to fear. One of the greatest gifts in A.A. for me has been the courage to take action, which I can do with God's help. After five years of sobriety I had to deal with a heavy dose of fear. God put the people in my life to help me do that and, through my working the Twelve Steps, I am becoming the whole person I wish to be and, for that, I am deeply grateful.

FEAR AND FAITH

The achievement of freedom from fear is a lifetime undertaking, one that can never be wholly completed. When under heavy attack, acute illness, or in other conditions of serious insecurity, we shall all react to this emotion—well or badly, as the case may be. Only the self-deceived will claim perfect freedom from fear.

AS BILL SEES IT, p. 263

Fear has caused suffering when I could have had more faith. There are times when fear suddenly tears me apart, just when I'm experiencing feelings of joy, happiness and a lightness of heart. Faith— and a feeling of self-worth toward a Higher Power —helps me endure tragedy and ecstasy. When I choose to give all of my fears over to my Higher Power, I will be free.

TODAY, I'M FREE

This brought me to the good healthy realization that there were plenty of situations left in the world over which I had no personal power—that if I was so ready to admit that to be the case with alcohol, so I must make the same admission with respect to much else. I would have to be still and know that He, not I, was God.

AS BILL SEES IT, p. 114

I am learning to practice acceptance in all circumstances of my life, so that I may enjoy peace of mind. At one time life was a constant battle because I felt I had to go through each day fighting myself, and everyone else. Eventually, this became a losing battle. I ended up getting drunk and crying over my misery. When I began to let go and let God take over my life I began to have peace of mind. Today, I am free. I do not have to fight anybody or anything anymore.

TRUSTING OTHERS

But does trust require that we be blind to other people's motives or, indeed, to our own? Not at all; this would be folly. Most certainly, we should assess the capacity for harm as well as the capability for good in every person that we would trust. Such a private inventory can reveal the degree of confidence we should extend in any given situation.

AS BILL SEES IT, p. 144

I am not a victim of others, but rather a victim of my expectations, choices and dishonesty. When I expect others to be what I want them to be and not who they are, when they fail to meet my expectations, I am hurt. When my choices are based on self-centeredness, I find I am lonely and distrustful. I gain confidence in myself, however, when I practice honesty in all my affairs. When I search my motives and am honest and trusting, I am aware of the capacity for harm in situations and can avoid those that are harmful.

A SPIRITUAL KINDERGARTEN

We are only operating a spiritual kindergarten in which people are enabled to get over drinking and find the grace to go on living to better effect.

AS BILL SEES IT, p. 95

When I came to A.A., I was run down by the bottle and wanted to lose the obsession to drink, but I didn't really know how to do that. I decided to stick around long enough to find out from the ones who went before me. All of a sudden I was thinking about God! I was told to get a Higher Power and I had no idea what one looked like. I found out there are many Higher Powers. I was told to find God, as I understand Him, that there was no doctrine of the Godhead in A.A. I found what worked for me and then asked that Power to restore me to sanity. The obsession to drink was removed and—one day at a time—my life went on, and I learned how to live sober.

A TWO-WAY STREET

If we ask, God will certainly forgive our derelictions.
But in no case does He render us white as snow and
keep us that way without our cooperation.

TWELVE STEPS AND TWELVE TRADITIONS, p. 65

When I prayed, I used to omit a lot of things for which I needed to be forgiven. I thought that if I didn't mention these things to God, He would never know about them. I did not know that if I had just forgiven myself for some of my past deeds, God would forgive me also. I was always taught to prepare for the journey through life, never realizing until I came to A.A.—when I honestly became willing to be taught forgiveness and forgiving—that life itself is the journey. The journey of life is a very happy one, as long as I am willing to accept change and responsibility.

A GIFT THAT GROWS WITH TIME

For most normal folks, drinking means conviviality, companionship and colorful imagination. It means release from care, boredom and worry. It is joyous intimacy with friends and a feeling that life is good.
ALCOHOLICS ANONYMOUS, p. 151

The longer I chased these elusive feelings with alcohol, the more out of reach they were. However, by applying this passage to my sobriety, I found that it described the magnificent new life made available to me by the A.A. program. "It" truly does "get better" one day at a time. The warmth, the love and the joy so simply expressed in these words grow in breadth and depth each time I read it. Sobriety is a gift that grows with time.

CONFORMING TO THE A.A. WAY

We obey A.A.'s Steps and Traditions because we really want them for ourselves. It is no longer a question of good or evil; we conform because we genuinely want to conform. Such is our process of growth in unity and function. Such is the evidence of God's grace and love among us.

A.A. COMES OF AGE, p. 106

It is fun to watch myself grow in A.A. I fought conformity to A.A. principles from the moment I entered, but I learned from the pain of my belligerence that, in choosing to live the A.A. way of life, I opened myself to God's grace and love. Then I began to know the full meaning of being a member of Alcoholics Anonymous.

THE DETERMINATION OF OUR
FOUNDERS

*A year and six months later these three had suc-
ceeded with seven more.*

ALCOHOLICS ANONYMOUS, p. 159

If it had not been for the fierce determination of our
founders, A.A. would have quickly faded like so
many other so-called good causes. I look at the
hundreds of meetings weekly in the city where I
live and I know A.A. is available twenty-four hours
a day. If I had had to hang on with nothing but
hope and a desire not to drink, experiencing rejection wherever I went, I would have sought the easier, softer way and returned to my previous way of
life.

A RIPPLING EFFECT

Having learned to live so happily, we'd show everyone else how. . . . Yes, we of A.A. did dream those dreams. How natural that was, since most alcoholics are bankrupt idealists. . . . So why shouldn't we share our way of life with everyone?
TWELVE STEPS AND TWELVE TRADITIONS, p. 156

The great discovery of sobriety led me to feel the need to spread the "good news" to the world around me. The grandiose thoughts of my drinking days returned. Later, I learned that concentrating on my own recovery was a full-time process. As I became a sober citizen in this world, I observed a rippling effect which, without any conscious effort on my part, reached any "related facility or outside enterprise," without diverting me from my primary purpose of staying sober and helping other alcoholics to achieve sobriety.

SACRIFICE = UNITY = SURVIVAL

The unity, the effectiveness, and even the survival of A.A. will always depend upon our continued willingness to give up some of our personal ambitions and desires for the common safety and welfare. Just as sacrifice means survival for the individual alcoholic, so does sacrifice mean unity and survival for the group and for A.A.'s entire Fellowship.

AS BILL SEES IT, p. 220

I have learned that I must sacrifice some of my personality traits for the good of A.A. and, as a result, I have been rewarded with many gifts. False pride can be inflated through prestige but, by living Tradition Six, I receive the gift of humility instead. Cooperation without affiliation is often deceiving. If I remain unrelated to outside interests, I am free to keep A.A. autonomous. Then the Fellowship will be here, healthy and strong for generations to come.

THE BEST FOR TODAY

The principles we have set down are guides to progress.

ALCOHOLICS ANONYMOUS, p. 60

Just as a sculptor will use different tools to achieve desired effects in creating a work of art, in Alcoholics Anonymous the Twelve Steps are used to bring about results in my own life. I do not overwhelm myself with life's problems, and how much more work needs to be done. I let myself be comforted in knowing that my life is now in the hands of my Higher Power, a master craftsman who is shaping each part of my life into a unique work of art. By working my program I can be satisfied, knowing that "in doing the best that we can for today, we are doing all that God asks of us."

THE HEART OF TRUE SOBRIETY

We find that no one need have difficulty with the spirituality of the program. Willingness, honesty and open-mindedness are the essentials of recovery. But these are indispensable.

ALCOHOLICS ANONYMOUS, p. 570

Am I honest enough to accept myself as I am and let this be the "me" that I let others see? Do I have the willingness to go to any length, to do whatever is necessary to stay sober? Do I have the open-mindedness to hear what I have to hear, to think what I have to think, and to feel what I have to feel?

If my answer to these questions is "Yes," I know enough about the spirituality of the program to stay sober. As I continue to work the Twelve Steps, I move on to the heart of true sobriety: serenity with myself, with others, and with God as I understand Him.

EXPERIENCE: THE BEST TEACHER

Being still inexperienced and having just made conscious contact with God, it is not probable that we are going to be inspired at all times.

ALCOHOLICS ANONYMOUS, p. 87

Some say that experience is the best teacher, but I believe that experience is the only teacher. I have been able to learn of God's love for me only by the experience of my dependence on that love. At first I could not be sure of His direction in my life, but now I see that if I am to be bold enough to ask for His guidance, I must act as if He has provided it. I frequently ask God to help me remember that He has a path for me.

A NATURAL FAITH

*. . . deep down in every man, woman and child, is
the fundamental idea of God. It may be obscured by
calamity, by pomp, by worship of other things, but in
some form or other it is there. For faith in a Power
greater than ourselves, and miraculous demonstra-
tions of that power in human lives, are facts as old as
man himself.*

ALCOHOLICS ANONYMOUS, p. 55

I have seen the workings of the unseen God in A.A.
rooms around the country. Miracles of recovery are
everywhere in evidence. I now believe that God is
in these rooms and in my heart. Today faith is as
natural to me, a former agnostic, as breathing, eating and sleeping. The Twelve Steps have helped to
change my life in many ways, but none is more
effective than the acquisition of a Higher Power.

A NEW DIRECTION

Our human resources, as marshalled by the will, were not sufficient; they failed utterly. . . . Every day is a day when we must carry the vision of God's will into all our activities.

ALCOHOLICS ANONYMOUS, pp. 45, 85

I hear talk of the "weak-willed" alcoholic, but I am one of the strongest-willed people on earth! I now know that my incredible strength of will is not enough to save my life. My problem is not one of "weakness," but rather of direction. When I, without falsely diminishing myself, accept my honest limitations and turn to God's guidance, my worst faults become my greatest assets. My strong will, rightly directed, keeps me working until the promises of the program become my daily reality.

IDENTIFYING FEAR . . .

The chief activator of our defects has been self-centered fear. . . .

TWELVE STEPS AND TWELVE TRADITIONS, p. 76

When I feel uncomfortable, irritated, or depressed, I look for fear. This "evil and corroding thread" is the root of my distress: Fear of failure; fear of others' opinions; fear of harm, and many other fears. I have found a Higher Power who does not want me to live in fear and, as a result, the experience of A.A. in my life is freedom and joy. I am no longer willing to live with the multitude of character defects that characterized my life while I was drinking. Step Seven is my vehicle to freedom from these defects. I pray for help in identifying the fear underneath the defect, and then I ask God to relieve me of that fear. This method works for me without fail and is one of the great miracles of my life in Alcoholics Anonymous.

. . . AND LETTING GO OF IT

. . . primarily fear that we would lose something we already possessed or would fail to get something we demanded. Living upon a basis of unsatisfied demands, we were in a state of continual disturbance and frustration. Therefore, no peace was to be had unless we could find a means of reducing these demands. The difference between a demand and a simple request is plain to anyone.
TWELVE STEPS AND TWELVE TRADITIONS, p. 76

Peace is possible for me only when I let go of expectations. When I'm trapped in thoughts about what I want and what should be coming to me, I'm in a state of fear or anxious anticipation and this is not conducive to emotional sobriety. I must surrender —over and over—to the reality of my dependence on God, for then I find peace, gratitude and spiritual security.

AN EVER-GROWING FREEDOM

The Seventh Step is where we make the change in our attitude which permits us, with humility as our guide, to move out from ourselves toward others and toward God.

TWELVE STEPS AND TWELVE TRADITIONS, p. 76

When I finally asked God to remove those things blocking me from Him and the sunlight of the Spirit, I embarked on a journey more glorious than I ever imagined. I experienced a freedom from those characteristics that had me wrapped up in myself. Because of this humbling Step, I feel clean.

I am especially aware of this Step because I'm now able to be useful to God and to my fellows. I know that He has granted me strength to do His bidding and has prepared me for anyone, and anything, that comes my way today. I am truly in His hands, and I give thanks for the joy that I can be useful today.

I AM AN INSTRUMENT

Humbly asked Him to remove our shortcomings.
TWELVE STEPS AND TWELVE TRADITIONS, p. 70

The subject of humility is a difficult one. Humility is not thinking less of myself than I ought to; it is acknowledging that I do certain things well, it is accepting a compliment graciously.

God can only do *for* me what He can do *through* me. Humility is the result of knowing that God is the doer, not me. In the light of this awareness, how can I take pride in my accomplishments? I am an instrument and any work I seem to be doing is being done by God through me. I ask God on a daily basis to remove my shortcomings, in order that I may more freely go about my A.A. business of "love and service."

TOWARD PEACE AND SERENITY

. . . when we have taken a square look at some of these defects, have discussed them with another, and have become willing to have them removed, our thinking about humility commences to have a wider meaning.

TWELVE STEPS AND TWELVE TRADITIONS, p. 74

When situations arise which destroy my serenity, pain often motivates me to ask God for clarity in seeing my part in the situation. Admitting my powerlessness, I humbly pray for acceptance. I try to see how my character defects contributed to the situation. Could I have been more patient? Was I intolerant? Did I insist on having my own way? Was I afraid? As my defects are revealed, I put self-reliance aside and humbly ask God to remove my shortcomings. The situation may not change, but as I practice exercising humility, I enjoy the peace and serenity which are the natural benefits of placing my reliance in a power greater than myself.

A TURNING POINT

A great turning point in our lives came when we sought for humility as something we really wanted, rather than as something we must have.

TWELVE STEPS AND TWELVE TRADITIONS, p. 75

Either the A.A. way of life becomes one of joy or I return to the darkness and despair of alcoholism. Joy comes to me when my attitude concerning God and humility turns to one of desire rather than of burden. The darkness in my life changes to radiant light when I arrive at the realization that being truthful and honest in dealing with my inventory results in my life being filled with serenity, freedom, and joy. Trust in my Higher Power deepens, and the flush of gratitude spreads through my being. I am convinced that being humble is being truthful and honest in dealing with myself and God. It is then that humility is something I "really want," rather than being "something I must have."

GIVING UP CENTER STAGE

For without some degree of humility, no alcoholic can stay sober at all. . . . Without it, they cannot live to much useful purpose, or, in adversity, be able to summon the faith that can meet any emergency.
TWELVE STEPS AND TWELVE TRADITIONS, p. 70

Why do I balk at the word "humility"? I am not humbling myself toward other people, but toward God, as I understand Him. Humility means "to show submissive respect," and by being humble I realize I am not the center of the universe. When I was drinking, I was consumed by pride and self-centeredness. I felt the entire world revolved around me, that I was master of my destiny. Humility enables me to depend more on God to help me overcome obstacles, to help me with my own imperfections, so that I may grow spiritually. I must solve more difficult problems to increase my proficiency and, as I encounter life's stumbling blocks, I must learn to overcome them through God's help. Daily communion with God demonstrates my humility and provides me with the realization that an entity more powerful than I is willing to help me if I cease trying to play God myself.

HUMILITY IS A GIFT

As long as we placed self-reliance first, a genuine reliance upon a Higher Power was out of the question. That basic ingredient of all humility, a desire to seek and do God's will, was missing.

TWELVE STEPS AND TWELVE TRADITIONS, p. 72

When I first came to A.A., I wanted to find some of the elusive quality called humility. I didn't realize I was looking for humility because I thought it would help me get what I wanted, and that I would do anything for others if I thought God would somehow reward me for it. I try to remember now that the people I meet in the course of my day are as close to God as I am ever going to get while on this earth. I need to pray for knowledge of God's will today, and see how my experience with hope and pain can help other people; if I can do that, I don't need to search for humility, it has found me.

A NOURISHING INGREDIENT

Where humility had formerly stood for a forced feeding on humble pie, it now begins to mean the nourishing ingredient which can give us serenity.
TWELVE STEPS AND TWELVE TRADITIONS, p. 74

How often do I focus on *my* problems and frustrations? When *I* am having a "good day" these same problems shrink in importance and my preoccupation with them dwindles. Wouldn't it be better if I could find a key to unlock the "magic" of my "good days" for use on the woes of my "bad days?"

I already *have* the solution! Instead of trying to run away from my pain and wish my problems away, I can pray for humility! Humility *will* heal the pain. Humility *will* take me out of myself. Humility, that strength granted to me by that "power greater than myself," is mine for the asking! Humility will bring balance back into my life. Humility will allow me to accept my humanness joyously.

PRIDE

For thousands of years we have been demanding more than our share of security, prestige, and romance. When we seemed to be succeeding, we drank to dream still greater dreams. When we were frustrated, even in part, we drank for oblivion. Never was there enough of what we thought we wanted.

In all these strivings, so many of them well-intentioned, our crippling handicap had been our lack of humility. We had lacked the perspective to see that character-building and spiritual values had to come first, and that material satisfactions were not the purpose of living.

TWELVE STEPS AND TWELVE TRADITIONS, p. 71

Time and again I approached the Seventh Step, only to fall back and regroup. Something was missing and the impact of the Step escaped me. What had I overlooked? A single word: read but ignored, the foundation of all the Steps, indeed the entire Alcoholics Anonymous program—that word is "humbly."

I understood my shortcomings: I constantly put tasks off; I angered easily; I felt too much self-pity; and I thought, why me? Then I remembered, "Pride goeth before the fall," and I eliminated pride from my life.

"A MEASURE OF HUMILITY"

In every case, pain had been the price of admission into a new life. But this admission price had purchased more than we expected. It brought a measure of humility, which we soon discovered to be a healer of pain.

TWELVE STEPS AND TWELVE TRADITIONS, p. 75

It was painful to give up trying to control my life, even though success eluded me, and when life got too rough, I drank to escape. Accepting life on life's terms will be mastered through the humility I experience when I turn my will and my life over to the care of God, as I understand Him. With my life in God's care, fear, uncertainty, and anger are no longer my response to those portions of life that I would rather not have happen to me. The pain of living through these times will be healed by the knowledge that I have received the spiritual strength to survive.

SURRENDER AND SELF-EXAMINATION

My stability came out of trying to give, not out of demanding that I receive.

Thus I think it can work out with emotional sobriety. If we examine every disturbance we have, great or small, we will find at the root of it some unhealthy dependency and its consequent unhealthy demand. Let us, with God's help, continually surrender these hobbling demands. Then we can be set free to live and love; we may then be able to Twelfth Step ourselves and others into emotional sobriety.

THE LANGUAGE OF THE HEART, p. 238

Years of dependency on alcohol as a chemical mood-changer deprived me of the capability to interact emotionally with my fellows. I thought I had to be self-sufficient, self-reliant, and self-motivated in a world of unreliable people. Finally I lost my self-respect and was left with dependency, lacking any ability to trust myself or to believe in anything. Surrender and self-examination while sharing with newcomers helped me to ask humbly for help.

GRATEFUL FOR WHAT I HAVE

During this process of learning more about humility, the most profound result of all was the change in our attitude toward God.

TWELVE STEPS AND TWELVE TRADITIONS, p 75

Today my prayers consist mostly of saying thank you to my Higher Power for my sobriety and for the wonder of God's abundance, but I need to ask also for help and the power to carry out His will for me. I no longer need God each minute to rescue me from the situations I get myself into by not doing His will. Now my gratitude seems to be directly linked to humility. As long as I have the humility to be grateful for what I have, God continues to provide for me.

FALSE PRIDE

Many of us who had thought ourselves religious awoke to the limitations of this attitude. Refusing to place God first, we had deprived ourselves of His help.

TWELVE STEPS AND TWELVE TRADITIONS, p. 75

Many false notions operate in false pride. The need for direction to live a decent life is satisfied by the hope experienced in the A.A. Fellowship. Those who have walked the way for years—a day at a time—say that a God-centered life has limitless possibilities for personal growth. This being so, much hope is transmitted by the elder A.A.s.

I thank my Higher Power for letting me know that He works through other people, and I thank Him for our trusted servants in the Fellowship who aid new members to reject their false ideals and to adopt those which lead to a life of compassion and trust. The elders in A.A. challenge the newcomers to "Come To"—so that they can "Come to Believe." I ask my Higher Power to help my unbelief.

SHORTCOMINGS REMOVED

But now the words "Of myself I am nothing, the Father doeth the works" began to carry bright promise and meaning.
TWELVE STEPS AND TWELVE TRADITIONS, p. 75

When I put the Seventh Step into action I must remember that there are no blanks to fill in. It doesn't say, "Humbly asked Him to (fill in the blank) remove our shortcomings." For years, I filled in the imaginary blank with "Help me!" "Give me the courage to," and "Give me the strength," etc. The Step says simply that God will remove my shortcomings. The only footwork I must do is "humbly ask," which for me means asking with the knowledge that of myself I am nothing, the Father within "doeth the works."

A PRICELESS GIFT

By this time in all probability we have gained some measure of release from our more devastating handicaps. We enjoy moments in which there is something like real peace of mind. To those of us who have hitherto known only excitement, depression, or anxiety—in other words, to all of us—this newfound peace is a priceless gift.

TWELVE STEPS AND TWELVE TRADITIONS, p. 74

I am learning to let go and let God, to have a mind that is open and a heart that is willing to receive God's grace in all my affairs; in this way I can experience the peace and freedom that come as a result of surrender. It has been proven that an act of surrender, originating in desperation and defeat, can grow into an ongoing act of faith, and that faith means freedom and victory.

"THE GOOD AND THE BAD"

"My Creator, I am now willing that you should have all of me, good and bad."

ALCOHOLICS ANONYMOUS, p. 76

The joy of life is in the giving. Being freed of my shortcomings, that I may more freely be of service, allows humility to grow in me. My shortcomings can be humbly placed in God's loving care and be removed. The essence of Step Seven is humility, and what better way to seek humility than by giving all of myself—good and bad—to God, so that He may remove the bad and return to me the good.

I ASK GOD TO DECIDE

"I pray that you now remove from me every single defect of character which stands in the way of my usefulness to you and my fellows."
ALCOHOLICS ANONYMOUS, p. 76

Having admitted my powerlessness and made a decision to turn my will and my life over to the care of God, as I understand Him, I don't decide which defects get removed, or the order in which defects get removed, or the time frame in which they get removed. I ask God to decide which defects stand in the way of my usefulness to Him and to others, and then I humbly ask Him to remove them.

HELPING OTHERS

Our very lives, as ex-problem drinkers, depend upon our constant thought of others and how we may help meet their needs.

ALCOHOLICS ANONYMOUS, p. 20

Self-centeredness was my problem. All my life people had been doing things for me and I not only expected it, but I was ungrateful and resentful they didn't do more. Why should I help others, when they were supposed to help me? If others had troubles, didn't they deserve them? I was filled with self-pity, anger and resentment. Then I learned that by helping others, with no thought of return, I could overcome this obsession with selfishness, and if I understood humility, I would know peace and serenity. No longer do I need to drink.

THOSE WHO STILL SUFFER

For us, if we neglect those who are still sick, there is unremitting danger to our own lives and sanity.
TWELVE STEPS AND TWELVE TRADITIONS, p. 151

I know the torment of drinking compulsively to quiet my nerves and my fears. I also know the pain of white-knuckled sobriety. Today, I do not forget the unknown person who suffers quietly, withdrawn and hiding in the desperate relief of drinking. I ask my Higher Power to give me His guidance and the courage to be willing to be His instrument to carry within me compassion and unselfish actions. Let the group continue to give me the strength to do with others what I cannot do alone.

THE "WORTH" OF SOBRIETY

Every A.A. group ought to be fully self-supporting, declining outside contributions.
TWELVE STEPS AND TWELVE TRADITIONS, p. 160

When I go shopping I look at the prices and if I need what I see, I buy it and pay. Now that I am supposed to be in rehabilitation, I have to straighten out my life. When I go to a meeting, I take a coffee with sugar and milk, sometimes more than one. But at the collection time, I am either too busy to take money out of my purse, or I do not have enough, but I am there because I *need* this meeting. I heard someone suggest dropping the price of a beer into the basket, and I thought, that's too much! I almost never give one dollar. Like many others, I rely on the more generous members to finance the Fellowship. I forget that it takes money to rent the meeting room, buy my milk, sugar and cups. I will pay, without hesitation, ninety cents for a cup of coffee at a restaurant after the meeting; I always have money for that. So, how much is my sobriety and my inner peace worth?

GIVING FREELY

We will make every personal sacrifice necessary to insure the unity of Alcoholics Anonymous. We will do this because we have learned to love God and one another. A.A. COMES OF AGE, p. 234

To be self-supporting through my own contributions was never a strong characteristic during my days as a practicing alcoholic. The giving of time or money always demanded a price tag.

As a newcomer I was told "we have to give it away in order to keep it." As I began to adopt the principles of Alcoholics Anonymous in my life, I soon found it was a privilege to give to the Fellowship as an expression of the gratitude I felt in my heart. My love of God and of others became the motivating factor in my life, with no thought of return. I realize now that giving freely is God's way of expressing Himself through me.

THOSE WHO STILL SUFFER

Let us resist the proud assumption that since God has enabled us to do well in one area we are destined to be a channel of saving grace for everybody.

A.A. COMES OF AGE, p. 232

A.A. groups exist to help alcoholics achieve sobriety. Large or small, firmly established or brand-new, speaker, discussion or study, each group has but one reason for being: to carry the message to the still-suffering alcoholic. The group exists so that the alcoholic can find a new way of life, a life abundant in happiness, joy, and freedom. To recover, most alcoholics need the support of a group of other alcoholics who share their experience, strength and hope. Thus my sobriety, and our program's survival, depend on my determination to put first things first.

ANONYMOUS GIFTS OF KINDNESS

As active alcoholics we were always looking for a handout in one way or another.
"THE TWELVE TRADITIONS ILLUSTRATED," p. 14

The challenge of the Seventh Tradition is a personal challenge, reminding me to share and give of myself. Before sobriety the only thing I ever supported was my habit of drinking. Now my efforts are a smile, a kind word, and kindness.

I saw that I had to start carrying my own weight and to allow my new friends to walk with me because, through the practice of the Twelve Steps and Twelve Traditions, I've never had it so good.

GIVING BACK

. . . he has struck something better than gold. . . .
He may not see at once that he has barely scratched
a limitless lode which will pay dividends only if he
mines it for the rest of his life and insists on giving
away the entire product.

ALCOHOLICS ANONYMOUS, p. 129

My part of the Seventh Tradition means so much more than just giving money to pay for the coffee. It means being accepted for myself by belonging to a group. For the first time I can be responsible, because I have a choice. I can learn the principles of working out problems in my daily life by getting involved in the "business" of A.A. By being self-supporting, I can give back to A.A. what A.A. gave to me! Giving back to A.A. not only ensures my own sobriety, but allows me to buy insurance that A.A. will be here for my grandchildren.

A PRAYER FOR ALL SEASONS

God grant us the serenity to accept the things we cannot change, Courage to change the things we can, And wisdom to know the difference.
TWELVE STEPS AND TWELVE TRADITIONS, p. 125

The power of this prayer is overwhelming in that its simple beauty parallels the A.A. Fellowship. There are times when I get stuck while reciting it, but if I examine the section which is troubling me, I find the answer to my problem. The first time this happened I was scared, but now I use it as a valuable tool. By accepting life as it is, I gain serenity. By taking action, I gain courage and I thank God for the ability to distinguish between those situations I can work on, and those I must turn over. All that I have now is a gift from God: my life, my usefulness, my contentment, and this program. The serenity enables me to continue walking forward.

Alcoholics Anonymous *is* the easier, softer way.

LIVING IT

The spiritual life is not a theory. We have to live it.
ALCOHOLICS ANONYMOUS, p. 83

When new in the program, I couldn't comprehend living the spiritual aspect of the program, but now that I'm sober, I can't comprehend living without it. Spirituality was what I had been seeking. God, as I understand Him, has given me answers to the whys that kept me drinking for twenty years. By living a spiritual life, by asking God for help, I have learned to love, care for and feel compassion for all my fellow men, and to feel joy in a world where, before, I felt only fear.

WE BECOME WILLING . . .

At the moment we are trying to put our lives in order. But this is not an end in itself.
ALCOHOLICS ANONYMOUS, p. 77

How easily I can become misdirected in approaching the Eighth Step! I wish to be free, somehow transformed by my Sixth and Seventh Step work. Now, more than ever, I am vulnerable to my own self-interest and hidden agenda. I am careful to remember that self-satisfaction, which sometimes comes through the spoken forgiveness of those I have harmed, is not my true objective. I become willing to make amends, knowing that through this process I am mended and made fit to move forward, to know and desire God's will for me.

. . . TO BE OF SERVICE

Our real purpose is to fit ourselves to be of maximum service to God and the people about us.
ALCOHOLICS ANONYMOUS, p. 77

It is clear that God's plan for me is expressed through love. God loved me enough to take me from alleys and jails so that I could be made a useful participant in His world. My response is to love all of His children through service and by example. I ask God to help me imitate His love for me through my love for others.

SEEDS OF FAITH

Faith, to be sure, is necessary, but faith alone can avail nothing. We can have faith, yet keep God out of our lives.

TWELVE STEPS AND TWELVE TRADITIONS, p. 34

As a child I constantly questioned the existence of God. To a "scientific thinker" like me, no answer could withstand a thorough dissection, until a very patient woman finally said to me, "You must have faith." With that simple statement, the seeds of my recovery were sown!

Today, as I practice my recovery—cutting back the weeds of alcoholism—slowly I am letting those early seeds of faith grow and bloom. Each day of recovery, of ardent gardening, brings the Higher Power of my understanding more fully into my life. My God has always been with me through faith, but it is my responsibility to have the willingness to accept His presence.

I ask God to grant me the willingness to do His will.

LISTENING DEEPLY

How persistently we claim the right to decide all by ourselves just what we shall think and just how we shall act.

TWELVE STEPS AND TWELVE TRADITIONS, p. 37

If I accept and act upon the advice of those who have made the program work for themselves, I have a chance to outgrow the limits of the past. Some problems will shrink to nothingness, while others may require patient, well-thought-out action. Listening deeply when others share can develop intuition in handling problems which arise unexpectedly. It is usually best for me to avoid impetuous action. Attending a meeting or calling a fellow A.A. member will usually reduce tension enough to bring relief to a desperate sufferer like me. Sharing problems at meetings with other alcoholics to whom I relate, or privately with my sponsor, can change aspects of the positions in which I find myself. Character defects are identified and I begin to see how they work against me. When I put my faith in the spiritual power of the program, when I trust others to teach me what I need to do to have a better life, I find that I can trust myself to do what is necessary.

DRIVEN

Driven by a hundred forms of fear, self-delusion, self-seeking, and self-pity, we step on the toes of our fellows and they retaliate.
ALCOHOLICS ANONYMOUS, p. 62

My selfishness was the driving force behind my drinking. I drank to celebrate success and I drank to drown my sorrows. Humility is the answer. I learn to turn my will and my life over to the care of God. My sponsor tells me that service keeps me sober. Today I ask myself: Have I sought knowledge of God's will for me? Have I done service for my A.A. group?

A "DESIGN FOR LIVING"

We in our turn, sought the same escape with all the desperation of drowning men. What seemed at first a flimsy reed, has proved to be the loving and powerful hand of God. A new life has been given us or, if you prefer, "a design for living" that really works.

ALCOHOLICS ANONYMOUS, p. 28

I try each day to raise my heart and hands in thanks to God for showing me a "design for living" that really works through our beautiful Fellowship. But what, exactly, *is* this "design for living" that "really works"? For me, it is the practice of the Twelve Steps to the best of my ability, the continued awareness of a God who loves me unconditionally, and the hope that, in each new day, there is a purpose for my being. I am truly, truly blessed in the Fellowship.

"MADE A LIST . . ."

Made a list of all persons we had harmed, . . .
TWELVE STEPS AND TWELVE TRADITIONS, p. 77

When I approached the Eighth Step, I wondered how I could list all the things that I have done to other people since there were so many people, and some of them weren't alive anymore. Some of the hurts I inflicted weren't bad, but they really bothered me. The main thing to see in this Step was to become willing to do whatever I had to do to make these amends to the best of my ability at that particular time. Where there is a will, there's a way, so if I want to feel better, I need to unload the guilt feelings I have. A peaceful mind has no room for feelings of guilt. With the help of my Higher Power, if I am honest with myself, I can cleanse my mind of these feelings.

". . . OF ALL PERSONS WE HAD HARMED"

. . . and became willing to make amends to them all.

TWELVE STEPS AND TWELVE TRADITIONS, p. 77

One of the key words in the Eighth Step is the word *all*. I am not free to select a few names for the list and to disregard others. It is a list of *all* persons I have harmed. I can see immediately that this Step entails forgiveness because if I'm not willing to forgive someone, there is little chance I will place his name on the list. Before I placed the first name on my list, I said a little prayer: "I forgive anyone and everyone who has ever harmed me at any time and under any circumstances."

It is well for me to contemplate a small, but very significant, two-letter word every time the Lord's Prayer is said. The word is *as*. I ask, "Forgive us our trespasses, *as* we forgive those who trespass against us." In this case, *as* means, "in the same manner." I am asking to be forgiven in the same manner that I forgive others. As I say this portion of the prayer, if I am harboring hatred or resentment, I am inviting more resentment, when I should be calling on the spirit of forgiveness.

REDOUBLING OUR EFFORTS

To a degree, he has already done this when taking moral inventory, but now the time has come when he ought to redouble his efforts to see how many people he has hurt, and in what ways.

TWELVE STEPS AND TWELVE TRADITIONS, p 77

As I continue to grow in sobriety, I become more aware of myself as a person of worth. In the process, I am better able to see others as persons, and with this comes the realization that these were people whom I had hurt in my drinking days. I didn't just lie, I lied about Tom. I didn't just cheat, I cheated Joe. What were seemingly impersonal acts, were really personal affronts, because it was people —people of worth—whom I had harmed. I need to do something about the people I have hurt so that I may enjoy a peaceful sobriety.

REMOVING "THE GROUND GLASS"

The moral inventory is a cool examination of the damages that occurred to us during life and a sincere effort to look at them in a true perspective. This has the effect of taking the ground glass out of us, the emotional substance that still cuts and inhibits.

AS BILL SEES IT, p. 140

My Eighth Step list used to drag me into a whirlpool of resentment. After four years of sobriety, I was blocked by denial connected with an ongoing abusive relationship. The argument between fear and pride eased as the words of the Step moved from my head to my heart. For the first time in years I opened my box of paints and poured out an honest rage, an explosion of reds and blacks and yellows. As I looked at the drawing, tears of joy and relief flowed down my cheeks. In my disease, I had given up my art, a self-inflicted punishment far greater than any imposed from outside. In my recovery, I learned that the pain of my defects is the very substance God uses to cleanse my character and to set me free.

A LOOK BACKWARD

First, we take a look backward and try to discover where we have been at fault; next we make a vigorous attempt to repair the damage we have done; . . .

TWELVE STEPS AND TWELVE TRADITIONS, p. 77

As a traveler on a fresh and exciting A.A. journey of recovery, I experienced a newfound peace of mind and the horizon appeared clear and bright, rather than obscure and dim. Reviewing my life to discover where I had been at fault seemed to be such an arduous and dangerous task. It was painful to pause and look backward. I was afraid I might stumble! Couldn't I put the past out of my mind and just live in my new golden present? I realized that those in the past whom I had harmed stood between me and my desire to continue my movement toward serenity. I had to ask for courage to face those persons from my life who still lived in my conscience, to recognize and deal with the guilt that their presence produced in me. I had to look at the damage I had done, and become willing to make amends. Only then could my journey of the spirit resume.

A CLEAN SWEEP

. . . and third, having thus cleaned away the debris of the past, we consider how, with our newfound knowledge of ourselves, we may develop the best possible relations with every human being we know.
TWELVE STEPS AND TWELVE TRADITIONS, p. 77

As I faced the Eighth Step, everything that was required for successful completion of the previous seven Steps came together: courage, honesty, sincerity, willingness and thoroughness. I could not muster the strength required for this task at the beginning, which is why this Step reads "Became willing. . . ."

I needed to develop the courage to begin, the honesty to see where I was wrong, a sincere desire to set things right, thoroughness in making a list, and willingness to take the risks required for true humility. With the help of my Higher Power in developing these virtues, I completed this Step and continued to move forward in my quest for spiritual growth.

REPAIRING THE DAMAGE

We attempt to sweep away the debris which has accumulated out of our effort to live on self-will and run the show ourselves. If we haven't the will to do this, we ask until it comes. Remember it was agreed at the beginning we would go to any lengths for victory over alcohol.

ALCOHOLICS ANONYMOUS, p. 76

Making a list of people I had harmed was not a particularly difficult thing to do. They had showed up in my Fourth Step inventory: people towards whom I had resentments, real or imagined, and whom I had hurt by acts of retaliation. For my recovery to be thorough, I believed it was not important for those who had legitimately harmed me to make amends to me. What is important in my relationship with God is that I stand before Him, knowing I have done what I can to repair the damage I have done.

DIDN'T WE HURT *ANYBODY?*

Some of us, though, tripped over a very different snag. We clung to the claim that when drinking we never hurt anybody but ourselves.
TWELVE STEPS AND TWELVE TRADITIONS, p. 79

This Step seemed so simple. I identified several people whom I had harmed, but they were no longer available. Still, I was uneasy about the Step and avoided conversations dealing with it. In time I learned to investigate those Steps and areas of my life which made me uncomfortable. My search revealed my parents, who had been deeply hurt by my isolation from them; my employer, who worried about my absences, my memory lapses, my temper; and the friends I had shunned, without explanation. As I faced the reality of the harm I had done, Step Eight took on new meaning. I am no longer uncomfortable and I feel clean and light.

"I HAD DROPPED OUT"

We might next ask ourselves what we mean when we say that we have "harmed" other people. What kinds of "harm" do people do one another, anyway? To define the word "harm" in a practical way, we might call it the result of instincts in collision, which cause physical, mental, emotional, or spiritual damage to people.

TWELVE STEPS AND TWELVE TRADITIONS, p. 80

I had been to Eighth Step meetings, always thinking, "I really haven't harmed many people, mostly myself." But the time came when I wrote my list out and it was not as short as I thought it would be. I either liked you, disliked you, or needed something from you—it was that simple. People hadn't done what I wanted them to do and intimate relationships were out of hand because of my partners' unreasonable demands. Were these "sins of omission"? Because of my drinking, I had "dropped out"—never sending cards, returning calls, being there for other people, or taking part in their lives. What a grace it has been to look at these relationships, to make my inventories in quiet, alone with the God of my understanding, and to go forth daily, with a willingness to be honest and forthright in my relationships.

RIGHTING THE HARM

In many instances we shall find that though the harm done others has not been great, the emotional harm we have done ourselves has.
TWELVE STEPS AND TWELVE TRADITIONS, p. 79

Have you ever thought that the harm you did a business associate, or perhaps a family member, was so slight that it really didn't deserve an apology because they probably wouldn't remember it anyway? If that person, and the wrong done to him, keeps coming to mind, time and again, causing an uneasy or perhaps guilty feeling, then I put that person's name at the top of my "amends list," and become willing to make a sincere apology, knowing I will feel calm and relaxed about that person once this very important part of my recovery is accomplished.

GETTING WELL

Very deep, sometimes quite forgotten, damaging emotional conflicts persist below the level of consciousness.

TWELVE STEPS AND TWELVE TRADITIONS, pp. 79-80

Only through positive action can I remove the remains of guilt and shame brought on by alcohol. Throughout my misadventures when I drank, my friends would say, "Why are you doing this? You're only hurting yourself." Little did I know how true were those words. Although I harmed others, some of my behavior caused grave wounds to my soul. Step Eight provides me with a way of forgiving myself. I alleviate much of the hidden damage when I make my list of those I have hurt. In making amends, I free myself of burdens, thus contributing to my healing.

A FRAME OF REFERENCE

Referring to our list [inventory] again. Putting out of our minds the wrongs others had done, we resolutely looked for our own mistakes. Where had we been selfish, dishonest, self-seeking and frightened?
ALCOHOLICS ANONYMOUS, p. 67

There is a wonderful freedom in not needing constant approval from colleagues at work or from the people I love. I wish I had known about this Step before, because once I developed a frame of reference, I felt able to do the next right thing, knowing that the action fit the situation and that it was the correct thing to do.

TOWARD EMOTIONAL FREEDOM

Since defective relations with other human beings have nearly always been the immediate cause of our woes, including our alcoholism, no field of investigation could yield more satisfying and valuable rewards than this one.
TWELVE STEPS AND TWELVE TRADITIONS, p. 80

Willingness is a peculiar thing for me in that, over a period of time, it seems to come, first with awareness, but then with a feeling of discomfort, making me want to take some action. As I reflected on taking the Eighth Step, my willingness to make amends to others came as a desire for forgiveness, of others and myself. I felt forgiveness toward others after I became aware of my part in the difficulties of relationships. I wanted to feel the peace and serenity described in the Promises. From working the first seven Steps, I became aware of whom I had harmed and that I had been my own worst enemy. In order to restore my relationships with my fellow human beings, I knew I would have to change. I wanted to learn to live in harmony with myself and others so that I could also live in emotional freedom. The beginning of the end to my isolation—from my fellows and from God—came when I wrote my Eighth Step list.

WE JUST TRY

My stability came out of trying to give, not out of demanding that I receive.

THE BEST OF BILL, pp. 46-47

As long as I try, with all my heart and soul, to pass along to others what has been passed along to me, and do not demand anything in return, life is good to me. Before entering this program of Alcoholics Anonymous I was never able to give without demanding something in return. Little did I know that, once I began to give freely of myself, I would begin to receive, without ever expecting or demanding anything at all. What I receive today is the gift of "stability," as Bill did: stability in my A.A. program; within myself; but most of all, in my relationship with my Higher Power, whom I choose to call God.

SEEKING EMOTIONAL STABILITY

When we developed still more, we discovered the best possible source of emotional stability to be God Himself. We found that dependence upon His perfect justice, forgiveness, and love was healthy, and that it would work where nothing else would. If we really depended upon God, we couldn't very well play God to our fellows nor would we feel the urge wholly to rely on human protection and care.

TWELVE STEPS AND TWELVE TRADITIONS, p. 116

All my life I depended on people for my emotional needs and security, but today I cannot live that way anymore. By the grace of God, I have admitted my powerlessness over people, places and things. I had been a real "people addict"; wherever I went there had to be someone who would pay some kind of attention to me. It was the kind of attitude that could only get worse, because the more I depended on others and demanded attention, the less I received.

I have given up believing that any human power can relieve me of that empty feeling. Although I remain a fragile human being who needs to work A.A.'s Steps to keep this particular principle before my personality, it is only a loving God who can give me inner peace and emotional stability.

BRINGING THE MESSAGE HOME

Can we bring the same spirit of love and tolerance into our sometimes deranged family lives that we bring to our A.A. group?
TWELVE STEPS AND TWELVE TRADITIONS, pp.111-12

My family members suffer from the effects of my disease. Loving and accepting them as they are— just as I love and accept A.A. members—fosters a return of love, tolerance and harmony to my life. Using common courtesy and respecting others' personal boundaries are necessary practices for all areas of my life.

A RIDDLE THAT WORKS

It may be possible to find explanations of spiritual experiences such as ours, but I have often tried to explain my own and have succeeded only in giving the story of it. I know the feeling it gave me and the results it has brought, but I realize I may never fully understand its deeper why and how.

AS BILL SEES IT, p. 313

I had a profound spiritual experience during an open A.A. meeting, which led me to blurt out, "I'm an alcoholic!" I have not had a drink since that day. I can tell you the words I heard just prior to my admission, and how those words affected me, but as to why it happened, I do not know. I believe a power greater than myself chose me to recover, yet I do not know why. I try not to worry or wonder about what I do not yet know; instead, I trust that if I continue to work the Steps, practice the A.A. principles in my life, and share my story, I will be guided lovingly toward a deep and mature spirituality in which more will be revealed to me. For the time being, it is a gift for me to trust God, work the Steps and help others.

THE GIFT OF BONDING

Relieve me of the bondage of self, that I may better do Thy will.

ALCOHOLICS ANONYMOUS, p. 63

Many times in my alcoholic state, I drank to establish a bond between myself and others, but I succeeded only in establishing the bondage of alcoholic loneliness. Through the A.A. way of life, I have received the gift of bonding—with those who were there before me, with those who are there now, and with those yet to come. For this gracious gift from God, I am forever grateful.

GIVING IT AWAY

Though they knew they must help other alcoholics if they would remain sober, that motive became secondary. It was transcended by the happiness they found in giving themselves to others.
ALCOHOLICS ANONYMOUS, p. 159

Those words, for me, refer to a transference of power, through which God, as I understand Him, enters my life. Through prayer and meditation, I open channels, then I establish and improve my conscious contact with God. Through action I then receive the power I need to maintain my sobriety each day. By maintaining my spiritual condition, by giving away what has been so freely given to me, I am granted a daily reprieve.

CENTERING OUR THOUGHTS

When World War II broke out, our A.A. dependence on a Higher Power had its first major test. A.A.'s entered the services and were scattered all over the world. Would they be able to take the discipline, stand up under fire, and endure . . . ?

AS BILL SEES IT, p. 200

I will center my thoughts on a Higher Power. I will surrender all to this power within me. I will become a soldier for this power, feeling the might of the spiritual army as it exists in my life today. I will allow a wave of spiritual union to connect me through my gratitude, obedience and discipline to this Higher Power. Let me allow this power to lead me through the orders of the day. May the steps I take today strengthen my words and deeds, may I know that the message I carry is mine to share, given freely by this power greater than myself.

LIGHTENING THE BURDEN

*Showing others who suffer how we were given help is
the very thing which makes life seem so worth while
to us now. . . . the dark past is . . . the key to life
and happiness for others.*

ALCOHOLICS ANONYMOUS, p. 124

Since I have been sober, I have been healed of many
pains: deceiving my partner, deserting my best
friend, and spoiling my mother's hopes for my life.
In each case someone in the program told me of a
similar problem, and I was able to share what happened to me. When my story was told, both of us
got up with lighter hearts.

I CHOOSE ANONYMITY

We are sure that humility, expressed by anonymity, is the greatest safeguard that Alcoholics Anonymous can ever have.

TWELVE STEPS AND TWELVE TRADITIONS, p. 187

Since there are no rules in A.A. I place myself where I want to be, and so I choose anonymity. I want my God to use me, humbly, as one of His tools in this program. Sacrifice is the art of giving of myself freely, allowing humility to replace my ego. With sobriety, I suppress that urge to cry out to the world, "I am a member of A.A." and I experience inner joy and peace. I let people see the changes in me and hope they will ask what happened to me. I place the principles of spirituality ahead of judging, fault-finding, and criticism. I want love and caring in my group, so I can grow.

THE ONLY REQUIREMENT . . .

"At one time . . . every A.A. group had many membership rules. Everybody was scared witless that something or somebody would capsize the boat. . . . The total list was a mile long. If all those rules had been in effect everywhere, nobody could have possibly joined A.A. at all, . . ."
TWELVE STEPS AND TWELVE TRADITIONS, pp. 139-40

I'm grateful that the Third Tradition only requires of me a desire to stop drinking. I had been breaking promises for years. In the Fellowship I didn't have to make promises, I didn't have to concentrate. It only required my attending one meeting, in a foggy condition, to know I was *home*. I didn't have to pledge undying love. Here, strangers hugged me. "It gets better," they said, and "One day at a time, you can do it." They were no longer strangers, but caring friends. I ask God to help me to reach out to people desiring sobriety, and to, please, keep me grateful!

A UNIQUE PROGRAM

Alcoholics Anonymous will never have a professional class. We have gained some understanding of the ancient words "Freely ye have received, freely give." We have discovered that at the point of professionalism, money and spirituality do not mix.

TWELVE STEPS AND TWELVE TRADITIONS, p. 166

I believe that Alcoholics Anonymous stands alone in the treatment of alcoholism because it is based solely on the principle of one alcoholic sharing with another alcoholic. This is what makes the program unique. When I decided that I wanted to stay sober, I called a woman who I knew was a sober member of A.A., and she carried the message of Alcoholics Anonymous to me. She received no monetary compensation, but rather was paid by staying sober another day herself. Today I could ask for no payment other than another day free from alcohol, so in that respect, I am generously paid for my labor.

WILLINGNESS TO GROW

If more gifts are to be received, our awakening has to go on.

AS BILL SEES IT, p. 8

Sobriety fills the painful "hole in the soul" that my alcoholism created. Often I feel so physically well that I believe my work is done. However, joy is not just the absence of pain; it is the gift of continued spiritual awakening. Joy comes from ongoing and active study, as well as application of the principles of recovery in my everyday life, and from sharing that experience with others. My Higher Power presents many opportunities for deeper spiritual awakening. I need only to bring into my recovery the willingness to grow. Today I am ready to grow.

FINDING "A REASON TO BELIEVE"

The willingness to grow is the essence of all spiritual development.

AS BILL SEES IT, p. 171

A line from a song goes, ". . . and I look to find a reason to believe . . ." It reminds me that at one time I was not able to find a reason to believe that my life was all right. Even though my life had been saved by my coming to A.A., three months later I went out and drank again. Someone told me: "You don't have to believe. Aren't you *willing* to believe that there is a reason for your life, even though you may not know yourself what that reason is, or that you may not sometimes know the right way to behave?" When I saw how willing I was to believe there *was* a reason for my life, then I could start to work on the Steps. Now when I begin with, "I am willing. . . ," I am using the key that leads to action, honesty, and an openness to a Higher Power moving through my life.

BUILDING A NEW LIFE

We feel a man is unthinking when he says sobriety is enough.
ALCOHOLICS ANONYMOUS, p. 82

When I reflect on Step Nine, I see that physical sobriety must be enough for me. I need to remember the hopelessness I felt before I found sobriety, and how I was willing to go to any lengths for it. Physical sobriety is not enough for those around me, however, since I must see that God's gift is used to build a new life for my family and loved ones. Just as importantly, I must be available to help others who want the A.A. way of life.

I ask God to help me share the gift of sobriety so that its benefits may be shown to those I know and love.

RECONSTRUCTION

Yes, there is a long period of reconstruction ahead. . . .

ALCOHOLICS ANONYMOUS, p. 83

The reconstruction of my life is the prime goal in my recovery as I avoid taking that first drink, one day at a time. The task is most successfully accomplished by working the Steps of our Fellowship. The spiritual life is not a theory; it works, but I have to live it. Step Two started me on my journey to develop a spiritual life; Step Nine allows me to move into the final phase of the initial Steps which taught me how to live a spiritual life. Without the guidance and strength of a Higher Power, it would be impossible to proceed through the various stages of reconstruction. I realize that God works for me and through me. Proof comes to me when I realize that God did for me what I could not do for myself, by removing that gnawing compulsion to drink. I must continue daily to seek God's guidance. He grants me a daily reprieve and will provide the power I need for reconstruction.

EMOTIONAL BALANCE

Made direct amends to such people wherever possible, . . .
TWELVE STEPS AND TWELVE TRADITIONS, p. 83

When I survey my drinking days, I recall many people whom my life touched casually, but whose days I troubled through my anger and sarcasm. These people are untraceable, and direct amends to them are not possible. The only amends I can make to those untraceable individuals, the only "changes for the better" I can offer, are indirect amends made to other people, whose paths briefly cross mine. Courtesy and kindness, regularly practiced, help me to live in emotional balance, at peace with myself.

REMOVING THREATS TO SOBRIETY

. . . except when to do so would injure them or others.

ALCOHOLICS ANONYMOUS, p. 59

Step Nine restores in me a feeling of belonging, not only to the human race but also to the everyday world. First, the Step makes me leave the safety of A.A., so that I may deal with non-A.A. people "out there," on their terms, not mine. It is a frightening but necessary action if I am to get back into life. Second, Step Nine allows me to remove threats to my sobriety by healing past relationships. Step Nine points the way to a more serene sobriety by letting me clear away past wreckage, lest it bring me down.

"OUR SIDE OF THE STREET"

We are there to sweep off our side of the street, realizing that nothing worth while can be accomplished until we do so, never trying to tell him what he should do. His faults are not discussed. We stick to our own.

ALCOHOLICS ANONYMOUS, pp. 77-78

I made amends to my dad soon after I quit drinking. My words fell on deaf ears since I had blamed him for my troubles. Several months later I made amends to my dad again. This time I wrote a letter in which I did not blame him nor mention his faults. It worked, and at last I understood! My side of the street is all that I'm responsible for and—thanks to God and A.A.—it's clean for today.

"WE ASKED HIS PROTECTION"

We asked His protection and care with complete abandon.

ALCOHOLICS ANONYMOUS, p. 59

I could not manage my life alone. I had tried that road and failed. My "ultimate sin" dragged me down to the lowest level I have ever reached and, unable even to function, I accepted the fact that I desperately needed help. I stopped fighting and surrendered entirely to God.

Only then did I start growing! God forgave me. A Higher Power had to have saved me, because the doctors doubted that I would survive. I have forgiven myself now and I enjoy a freedom I have never before experienced. I've opened my heart and mind to Him. The more I learn, the less I know—a humbling fact—but I sincerely want to keep growing. I enjoy serenity, but only when I entrust my life totally to God. As long as I am honest with myself and ask for His help, I can maintain this rewarding existence.

Just for today, I strive to live His will for me—soberly.

I thank God that today I can choose not to drink.

Today, life is beautiful!

OPENING NEW DOORS

They [the Promises] are being fulfilled among us—
sometimes quickly, sometimes slowly.
ALCOHOLICS ANONYMOUS, p. 84

The Promises talked about in this passage are slowly coming to life for me. What has given me hope is putting Step Nine into action. The Step has allowed me to see and set goals for myself in recovery.

Old habits and behaviors die hard. Working Step Nine enables me to close the door on the drunk I was, and to open new avenues for myself as a sober alcoholic. Making direct amends is crucial for me. As I repair relationships and behavior of the past, I am better able to live a sober life!

Although I have some years of sobriety, there are times when the "old stuff" from the past needs to be taken care of, and Step Nine always works, when I work it.

RECOVERY BY PROXY?

They [the Promises] will always materialize if we work for them.

ALCOHOLICS ANONYMOUS, p. 84

Sometimes I think: "Making these amends is going too far! No one should have to humble himself like that!" However, it is this very humbling of myself that brings me that much closer to the sunlight of the spirit. A.A. is the only hope I have if I am to continue healing and gain a life of happiness, friendship and harmony.

MAKING AMENDS

Above all, we should try to be absolutely sure that we are not delaying because we are afraid.
TWELVE STEPS AND TWELVE TRADITIONS, p. 87

To have courage, to be unafraid, are gifts of my recovery. They empower me to ask for help and to go forth in making my amends with a sense of dignity and humility. Making amends may require a certain amount of honesty that I feel I lack, yet with the help of God and the wisdom of others, I can reach within and find the strength to act. My amends may be accepted, or they may not, but after they are completed I can walk with a sense of freedom and know that, for today, I am responsible.

I AM RESPONSIBLE

For the readiness to take the full consequences of our past acts, and to take responsibility for the well-being of others at the same time, is the very spirit of Step Nine.

TWELVE STEPS AND TWELVE TRADITIONS, p. 87

In recovery, and through the help of Alcoholics Anonymous, I learn that the very thing I fear is my freedom. It comes from my tendency to recoil from taking responsibility for anything: I deny, I ignore, I blame, I avoid. Then one day, I look, I admit, I accept. The freedom, the healing and the recovery I experience is in the looking, admitting and accepting. I learn to say, "Yes, I am responsible." When I can speak those words with honesty and sincerity, then I am free.

REPAIRING THE DAMAGE

Good judgment, a careful sense of timing, courage and prudence—these are the qualities we shall need when we take Step Nine.

TWELVE STEPS AND TWELVE TRADITIONS, p. 83

To make amends can be viewed two ways: first, that of repairing damage, for if I have damaged my neighbor's fence, I "make a mend," and that is a direct amend; the second way is by modifying my behavior, for if my actions have harmed someone, I make a daily effort to cause no further harm. I "mend my ways," and that is an indirect amend. Which is the best approach? The only right approach, provided that I am causing no further harm in so doing, is to do both. If harm is done, then I simply "mend my ways." To take action in this manner assures me of making honest amends.

PEACE OF MIND

Do we lay the matter before our sponsor or spiritual adviser, earnestly asking God's help and guidance— meanwhile resolving to do the right thing when it becomes clear, cost what it may?
TWELVE STEPS AND TWELVE TRADITIONS, pp. 86-87

My belief in a Higher Power is an essential part of my work on Step Nine; forgiveness, timing, and right motives are the other ingredients. My willingness to do the Step is a growing experience that opens the door for new and honest relationships with the people I have harmed. My responsible action brings me closer to the spiritual principles of the program—love and service. Peace of mind, serenity, and a stronger faith are sure to follow.

A NEW LIFE

Yes, there is a substitute and it is vastly more than that. It is a fellowship in Alcoholics Anonymous. . . . Life will mean something at last.
ALCOHOLICS ANONYMOUS, p. 152

Life is better without alcohol. A.A. and the presence of a Higher Power keeps me sober, but the grace of God does even better; it brings service into my life. Contact with the A.A. program teaches me a new and greater understanding of what Alcoholics Anonymous is and what it does, but most importantly, it helps to show me who I am: an alcoholic who needs the constant experience of the Alcoholics Anonymous program so that I may live a life given to me by my Higher Power.

WE STAND—OR FALL—TOGETHER

. . . no society of men and women ever had a more urgent need for continuous effectiveness and permanent unity. We alcoholics see that we must work together and hang together, else most of us will finally die alone.

ALCOHOLICS ANONYMOUS, p. 563

Just as the Twelve Steps of A.A. are written in a specific sequence for a reason, so it is with the Twelve Traditions. The First Step and the First Tradition attempt to instill in me enough humility to allow me a chance at survival. Together they are the basic foundation upon which the Steps and Traditions that follow are built. It is a process of ego deflation which allows me to grow as an individual through the Steps, and as a contributing member of a group through the Traditions. Full acceptance of the First Tradition allows me to set aside personal ambitions, fears and anger when they are in conflict with the common good, thus permitting me to work with others for our mutual survival. Without Tradition One I stand little chance of maintaining the unity required to work with others effectively, and I also stand to lose the remaining Traditions, the Fellowship, and my life.

FREEDOM FROM FEAR

When, with God's help, we calmly accepted our lot, then we found we could live at peace with ourselves and show others who still suffered the same fears that they could get over them, too. We found that freedom from fear was more important than freedom from want.

TWELVE STEPS AND TWELVE TRADITIONS, p. 122

Material values ruled my life for many years during my active alcoholism. I believed that all of my possessions would make me happy, yet I still felt bankrupt after I obtained them. When I first came into A.A., I found out about a new way of living. As a result of learning to trust others, I began to believe in a power greater than myself. Having faith freed me from the bondage of self. As material gains were replaced by the gifts of the spirit, my life became manageable. I then chose to share my experiences with other alcoholics.

LOVED BACK TO RECOVERY

Our whole treasured philosophy of self-sufficiency had to be cast aside. This had not been done with old-fashioned willpower; it was instead a matter of developing the willingness to accept *these new facts of living. We neither ran nor fought. But* accept *we did. And then we were free.*

BEST OF THE GRAPEVINE, Vol. I, p. 198

I can be free of my old enslaving self. After a while I recognize, and believe in, the good within myself. I see that I have been loved back to recovery by my Higher Power, who envelops me. My Higher Power becomes that source of love and strength that is performing a continuing miracle in me. I am sober . . . and I am grateful.

ACCEPTANCE

We admitted we couldn't lick alcohol with our own remaining resources, and so we accepted the further fact that dependence upon a Higher Power (if only our A.A. group) could do this hitherto impossible job. The moment we were able to accept these facts fully, our release from the alcohol compulsion had begun.

AS BILL SEES IT, p. 109

Freedom came to me only with my acceptance that I could turn my will and my life over to the care of my Higher Power, whom I call God. Serenity seeped into the chaos of my life when I accepted that what I was going through was life, and that God would help me through my difficulties—and much more, as well. Since then He has helped me through all of my difficulties! When I accept situations as they are, not as I wish them to be, then I can begin to grow and have serenity and peace of mind.

H.P. AS GUIDE

See to it that your relationship with Him is right, and great events will come to pass for you and countless others. This is the Great Fact for us.

ALCOHOLICS ANONYMOUS, p. 164

Having a right relationship with God seemed to be an impossible order. My chaotic past had left me filled with guilt and remorse and I wondered how this "God business" could work. A.A. told me that I must turn my will and my life over to the care of God, as I understand Him. With nowhere else to turn, I went down on my knees and cried, "God, I can't do this. Please help me!" It was when I admitted my powerlessness that a glimmer of light began to touch my soul, and then a willingness emerged to let God control my life. With Him as my guide, great events began to happen, and I found the beginning of sobriety.

THE LAST PROMISE

We will suddenly realize that God is doing for us what we could not do for ourselves.

ALCOHOLICS ANONYMOUS, p. 84

The last Promise in the Big Book came true for me on the very first day of sobriety. God kept me sober that day, and on every other day I allowed Him to operate in my life. He gives me the strength, courage and guidance to meet my responsibilities in life so that I am then able to reach out and help others stay sober and grow. He manifests within me, making me a channel of His word, thought and deed. He works with my inner self, while I produce in the outer world, for He will not do for me what I can do for myself. I must be willing to do His work, so that He can function through me successfully.

A "LIMITLESS LODE"

Like a gaunt prospector, belt drawn in over the last ounce of food, our pick struck gold. Joy at our release from a lifetime of frustration knew no bounds. Father feels he has struck something better than gold. For a time he may try to hug the new treasure to himself. He may not see at once that he has barely scratched a limitless lode which will pay dividends only if he mines it for the rest of his life and insists on giving away the entire product.

ALCOHOLICS ANONYMOUS, pp. 128-29

When I talk with a newcomer to A.A., my past looks me straight in the face. I see the pain in those hopeful eyes, I extend my hand, and then the miracle happens: *I* become healed. My problems vanish as I reach out to this trembling soul.

"I WAS AN EXCEPTION"

He [Bill W.] said to me, gently and simply, "Do you think that you are one of us?"
ALCOHOLICS ANONYMOUS, p. 413

During my drinking life I was convinced I was an exception. I thought I was beyond petty requirements and had the right to be excused. I never realized that the dark counterbalance of my attitude was the constant feeling that I did not "belong." At first, in A.A., I identified with others only as an alcoholic. What a wonderful awakening for me it has been to realize that, if human beings were doing the best they could, then so was I! All of the pains, confusions and joys they feel are not exceptional, but part of my life, just as much as anybody's.

VIGILANCE

We have seen the truth demonstrated again and again: "Once an alcoholic, always an alcoholic." Commencing to drink after a period of sobriety, we are in a short time as bad as ever. If we are planning to stop drinking, there must be no reservation of any kind, nor any lurking notion that someday we will be immune to alcohol.

ALCOHOLICS ANONYMOUS, p. 33

Today I am an alcoholic. Tomorrow will be no different. My alcoholism lives within me now and forever. I must never forget what I am. Alcohol will surely kill me if I fail to recognize and acknowledge my disease on a daily basis. I am not playing a game in which a loss is a temporary setback. I am dealing with my disease, for which there is no cure, only daily acceptance and vigilance.

FIRST THINGS FIRST

Some of us have taken very hard knocks to learn this truth: Job or no job—wife or no wife—we simply do not stop drinking so long as we place dependence upon other people ahead of dependence on God.

ALCOHOLICS ANONYMOUS, p. 98

Before coming to A.A., I always had excuses for taking a drink: "She said . . . ," "He said . . . ," "I got fired yesterday," "I got a great job today." No area of my life could be good if I drank again. In sobriety my life gets better each day. I must always remember not to drink, to trust God, and to stay active in A.A. Am I putting anything before my sobriety, God, and A.A. today?

OUR CHILDREN

The alcoholic may find it hard to re-establish friendly relations with his children. . . . In time they will see that he is a new man and in their own way they will let him know it. . . . From that point on, progress will be rapid. Marvelous results often follow such a reunion.

ALCOHOLICS ANONYMOUS, p. 134

While on the road to recovery I received a gift that could not be purchased. It was a card from my son in college, saying, "Dad, you can't imagine how glad I am that everything is okay. Happy Birthday, I love you." My son had told me that he loved me before. It had been during the previous Christmas holidays, when he had said to me, while crying, "Dad, I love you! Can't you see what you're doing to yourself?" I couldn't. Choked with emotion, I had cried, but this time, when I received my son's card, my tears were tears of joy, not desperation.

WITHOUT RESERVATION

When brimming with gratitude, one's heartbeat must surely result in outgoing love, . . .
AS BILL SEES IT, p. 37

While practicing service to others, if my successes give rise to grandiosity, I must reflect on what brought me to this point. What has been given joyfully, with love, must be passed on without reservation and without expectation. For as I grow, I find that no matter how much I give with love, I receive much more in spirit.

LOVE WITHOUT STRINGS

Practical experience shows that nothing will so much insure immunity from drinking as intensive work with other alcoholics.

ALCOHOLICS ANONYMOUS, p. 89

Sponsorship held two surprises for me. First, that my sponsees cared about me. What I had thought was gratitude was more like love. They wanted me to be happy, to grow and remain sober. Knowing how they felt kept me from drinking more than once. Second, I discovered that I was able to love someone else responsibly, with respectful and genuine concern for that person's growth. Before that time, I had thought that my ability to care sincerely about another's well-being had atrophied from lack of use. To learn that I can love, without greed or anxiety, has been one of the deepest gifts the program has given me. Gratitude for that gift has kept me sober many times.

EXACTLY ALIKE

Frequent contact with newcomers and with each other is the bright spot of our lives.

ALCOHOLICS ANONYMOUS, p. 89

A man came to the meeting drunk, interrupted the speakers, stood up and took his shirt off, staggered loudly back and forth for coffee, demanded to talk, and eventually called the group's secretary an unquotable name and walked out. I was glad he was there—once again I saw what I had been like. But I also saw what I still am, and what I still could be. I don't have to be drunk to want to be the exception and the center of attention. I have often felt abused and responded abusively when I was simply being treated as a garden variety human being. The more the man tried to insist he was different, the more I realized that he and I were exactly alike.

THE CIRCLE AND THE TRIANGLE

The circle stands for the whole world of A.A., and the triangle stands for A.A.'s Three Legacies of Recovery, Unity, and Service. Within our wonderful new world, we have found freedom from our fatal obsession.

A.A. COMES OF AGE, p. 139

Early in my A.A. life, I became employed in its services and I found the explanation of our society's logo to be very appropriate. First, a circle of love and service with a well-balanced triangle inside, the base of which represents our Recovery through the Twelve Steps. Then the other two sides, representing Unity and Service, respectively. The three sides of the triangle are equal. As I grew in A.A. I soon identified myself with this symbol. I am the circle, and the sides of the triangle represent three aspects of my personality: physical, emotional sanity, spirituality, the latter forming the symbol's base. Taken together, all three aspects of my personality translate into a sober and happy life.

LEST WE BECOME COMPLACENT

It is easy to let up on the spiritual program of action and rest on our laurels. We are headed for trouble if we do, for alcohol is a subtle foe.
ALCOHOLICS ANONYMOUS, p. 85

When I am in pain it is easy to stay close to the friends I have found in the program. Relief from that pain is provided in the solutions contained in A.A.'s Twelve Steps. But when I am feeling good and things are going well, I can become complacent. To put it simply, I become lazy and turn into the problem instead of the solution. I need to get into action, to take stock: where am I and where am I going? A daily inventory will tell me what I must change to regain spiritual balance. Admitting what I find within myself, to God and to another human being, keeps me honest and humble.

"THE ACID TEST"

As we work the first nine Steps, we prepare ourselves for the adventure of a new life. But when we approach Step Ten we commence to put our A.A. way of living to practical use, day by day, in fair weather or foul. Then comes the acid test: can we stay sober, keep in emotional balance, and live to good purpose under all conditions?

TWELVE STEPS AND TWELVE TRADITIONS, p. 88

I know the Promises are being fulfilled in my life, but I want to maintain and develop them by the daily application of Step Ten. I have learned through this Step that if I am disturbed, there is something wrong with me. The other person may be wrong too, but I can only deal with my feelings. When I am hurt or upset, I have to continually look for the cause in me, and then I have to admit and correct my mistakes. It isn't easy, but as long as I know I am progressing spiritually, I know that I can mark my effort up as a job well done. I have found that pain is a friend; it lets me know there is something wrong with my emotions, just as a physical pain lets me know there is something wrong with my body. When I take the appropriate action through the Twelve Steps, the pain gradually goes away.

SERENITY AFTER THE STORM

Someone who knew what he was talking about once remarked that pain was the touchstone of all spiritual progress. How heartily we A.A.'s can agree with him. . . .

TWELVE STEPS AND TWELVE TRADITIONS, pp. 93-94

When on the roller coaster of emotional turmoil, I remember that growth is often painful. My evolution in the A.A. program has taught me that I must experience the inner change, however painful, that eventually guides me from selfishness to selflessness. If I am to have serenity, I must STEP my way past emotional turmoil and its subsequent hangover, and be grateful for continuing spiritual progress.

A NECESSARY PRUNING

. . . we know that the pains of drinking had to come before sobriety, and emotional turmoil before serenity.
TWELVE STEPS AND TWELVE TRADITIONS, p. 94

I love spending time in my garden feeding and pruning my beautiful flowers. One day, as I was busily snipping away, a neighbor stopped by. She commented, "Oh! Your plants are so beautiful, it seems such a shame to cut them back." I replied, "I know how you feel, but the excess must be removed so they can grow stronger and healthier." Later I thought that perhaps my plants feel pain, but God and I know it's part of the plan and I've seen the results. I was quickly reminded of my precious A.A. program and how we all grow through pain. I ask God to prune me when it's time, so I can grow.

YESTERDAY'S BAGGAGE

For the wise have always known that no one can make much of his life until self-searching becomes a regular habit, until he is able to admit and accept what he finds, and until he patiently and persistently tries to correct what is wrong.

TWELVE STEPS AND TWELVE TRADITIONS, p. 88

I have more than enough to handle today, without dragging along yesterday's baggage too. I must balance today's books, if I am to have a chance tomorrow. So I ask myself if I have erred and how I can avoid repeating that particular behavior. Did I hurt anyone, did I help anyone, and why? Some of today is bound to spill over into tomorrow, but most of it need not if I make an honest daily inventory.

FACING OURSELVES

. . . and Fear says, "You dare not look!"
TWELVE STEPS AND TWELVE TRADITIONS, p. 49

How often I avoided a task in my drinking days just because it appeared so large! Is it any wonder, even if I have been sober for some time, that I will act that same way when faced with what appears to be a monumental job, such as a searching and fearless moral inventory of myself? What I discover after I have arrived at the other side—when my inventory is completed—is that the illusion was greater than the reality. The fear of facing myself kept me at a standstill and, until I became willing to put pencil to paper, I was arresting my growth based on an intangible.

DAILY MONITORING

Continued to take personal inventory. . . .
TWELVE STEPS AND TWELVE TRADITIONS, p. 88

The spiritual axiom referred to in the Tenth Step— "every time we are disturbed, no matter what the cause, there is something wrong *with us*"—also tells me that there are no exceptions to it. No matter how unreasonable others may seem, I am responsible for not reacting negatively. Regardless of what is happening around me I will always have the prerogative, and the responsibility, of choosing what happens within me. I am the creator of my own reality.

When I take my daily inventory, I know that I must stop judging others. If I judge others, I am probably judging myself. Whoever is upsetting me most is my best teacher. I have much to learn from him or her, and in my heart, I should thank that person.

DAILY INVENTORY

. . . and when we were wrong promptly admitted it.
ALCOHOLICS ANONYMOUS, p. 59

I was beginning to approach my new life of sobriety with unaccustomed enthusiasm. New friends were cropping up and some of my battered friendships had begun to be repaired. Life was exciting, and I even began to enjoy my work, becoming so bold as to issue a report on the lack of proper care for some of our clients. One day a co-worker informed me that my boss was really sore because a complaint, submitted over his head, had caused him much discomfort at the hands of his superiors. I knew that my report had created the problem, and began to feel responsible for my boss's difficulty. In discussing the affair, my co-worker tried to reassure me that an apology was not necessary, but I soon became convinced that I had to do something, regardless of how it might turn out. When I approached my boss and owned up to my hand in his difficulties, he was surprised. But unexpected things came out of our encounter, and my boss and I were able to agree to interact more directly and effectively in the future.

A SPIRITUAL AXIOM

It is a spiritual axiom that every time we are disturbed, no matter what the cause, there is something wrong with us.

TWELVE STEPS AND TWELVE TRADITIONS, p. 90

I never truly understood the Tenth Step's spiritual axiom until I had the following experience. I was sitting in my bedroom, reading into the wee hours, when suddenly I heard my dogs barking in the back yard. My neighbors frown on this kind of disturbance so, with mixed feelings of anger and shame, as well as fear of my neighbors' disapproval, I immediately called in my dogs. Several weeks later the exact situation repeated itself but this time, because I was feeling more at peace with myself, I was able to accept the situation—dogs *will* bark—and I calmly called in the dogs. Both incidents taught me that when a person experiences nearly identical events and reacts two different ways, then it is not the event which is of prime importance, but the person's spiritual condition. Feelings come from inside, not from outward circumstances. When my spiritual condition is positive, I react positively.

FIXING ME, NOT YOU

If somebody hurts us and we are sore, we are in the wrong also.

TWELVE STEPS AND TWELVE TRADITIONS, p. 90

What a freedom I felt when this passage was pointed out to me! Suddenly I saw that I could do something about my anger, I could fix me, instead of trying to fix *them.* I believe that there are no exceptions to the axiom. When I am angry, my anger is always self-centered. I must keep reminding myself that I am human, that I am doing the best I can, even when that best is sometimes poor. So I ask God to remove my anger and truly set me free.

SELF-RESTRAINT

Our first objective will be the development of self-restraint.

TWELVE STEPS AND TWELVE TRADITIONS, p. 91

My drive to work provides me with an opportunity for self-examination. One day while making this trip, I began to review my progress in sobriety, and was not happy with what I saw. I hoped that, as the work day progressed, I would forget these troublesome thoughts, but as one disappointment after another kept coming, my discontent only increased, and the pressures within me kept mounting.

I retreated to an isolated table in the lounge, and asked myself how I could make the most of the rest of the day. In the past, when things went wrong, I instinctively wanted to fight back. But during the short time I had been trying to live the A.A. program I had learned to step back and take a look at myself. I recognized that, although I was not the person I wanted to be, I had learned to not react in my old ways. Those old patterns of behavior only brought sorrow and hurt, to me and to others. I returned to my work station, determined to make the day a productive one, thanking God for the chance to make progress that day.

CURBING RASHNESS

When we speak or act hastily or rashly, the ability to be fair-minded and tolerant evaporates on the spot.
TWELVE STEPS AND TWELVE TRADITIONS, p. 91

Being fair-minded and tolerant is a goal toward which I must work daily. I ask God, as I understand Him, to help me to be loving and tolerant to my loved ones, and to those with whom I am in close contact. I ask for guidance to curb my speech when I am agitated, and I take a moment to reflect on the emotional upheaval my words may cause, not only to someone else, but also to myself. Prayer, meditation and inventories are the key to sound thinking and positive action for me.

UNREMITTING INVENTORIES

Continue to watch for selfishness, dishonesty, resentment, and fear. When these crop up, we ask God at once to remove them. We discuss them with someone immediately and make amends quickly if we have harmed anyone. Then we resolutely turn our thoughts to someone we can help.

ALCOHOLICS ANONYMOUS, p. 84

The immediate admission of wrong thoughts or actions is a tough task for most human beings, but for recovering alcoholics like me it is difficult because of my propensity toward ego, fear and pride. The freedom the A.A. program offers me becomes more abundant when, through unremitting inventories of myself, I admit, acknowledge and accept responsibility for my wrong-doing. It is possible then for me to grow into a deeper and better understanding of humility. My willingness to admit when the fault is mine facilitates the progression of my growth and helps me to become more understanding and helpful to others.

A PROGRAM FOR LIVING

When we retire at night, we constructively review our day. . . . On awakening let us think about the twenty-four hours ahead. . . . Before we begin, we ask God to direct our thinking, especially asking that it be divorced from self-pity, dishonest or self-seeking motives.

ALCOHOLICS ANONYMOUS, p. 86

I lacked serenity. With more to do than seemed possible, I fell further behind, no matter how hard I tried. Worries about things not done yesterday and fear of tomorrow's deadlines denied me the calm I needed to be effective each day. Before taking Steps Ten and Eleven, I began to read passages like the one cited above. I tried to focus on God's will, not my problems, and to trust that He would manage my day. It worked! Slowly, but it worked!

MY CHECKLIST, NOT YOURS

Gossip barbed with our anger, a polite form of murder by character assassination, has its satisfactions for us, too. Here we are not trying to help those we criticize; we are trying to proclaim our own righteousness.

TWELVE STEPS AND TWELVE TRADITIONS, p. 67

Sometimes I don't realize that I gossiped about someone until the end of the day, when I take an inventory of the day's activities, and then, my gossiping appears like a blemish in my beautiful day. How could I have said something like that? Gossip shows its ugly head during a coffee break or lunch with business associates, or I may gossip during the evening, when I'm tired from the day's activities, and feel justified in bolstering my ego at the expense of someone else.

Character defects like gossip sneak into my life when I am not making a constant effort to work the Twelve Steps of recovery. I need to remind myself that my uniqueness is the blessing of my being, and that applies equally to everyone who crosses my path in life's journey. Today the only inventory I need to take is my own. I'll leave judgment of others to the Final Judge—Divine Providence.

THROUGHOUT EACH DAY

This is not an overnight matter. It should continue for our lifetime.

ALCOHOLICS ANONYMOUS, p. 84

During my early years in A.A. I saw Step Ten as a suggestion that I periodically look at my behavior and reactions. If there was something wrong, I should admit it; if an apology was necessary, I should give one. After a few years of sobriety I felt I should undertake a self-examination more frequently. Not until several more years of sobriety had elapsed did I realize the full meaning of Step Ten, and the word "continued." "Continued" does not mean occasionally, or frequently. It means *throughout* each day.

A DAILY TUNE-UP

Every day is a day when we must carry the vision of God's will into all of our activities.

ALCOHOLICS ANONYMOUS, p. 85

How do I maintain my spiritual condition? For me it's quite simple: on a daily basis I ask my Higher Power to grant me the gift of sobriety for that day! I have talked to many alcoholics who have gone back to drinking and I always ask them: "Did you pray for sobriety the day you took your first drink?" Not one of them said yes. As I practice Step Ten and try to keep my house in order on a daily basis, I have the knowledge that if I ask for a daily reprieve, it will be granted.

AN OPEN MIND

True humility and an open mind can lead us to faith, . . .

TWELVE STEPS AND TWELVE TRADITIONS, p. 33

My alcoholic thinking led me to believe that I could control my drinking, but I couldn't. When I came to A.A., I realized that God was speaking to me through my group. My mind was open just enough to know that I needed His help. A real, honest acceptance of A.A. took more time, but with it came humility. I know how insane I was, and I am extremely grateful to have my sanity restored to me and to be a sober alcoholic. The new, sober me is a much better person than I ever could have been without A.A.

A.A'S "MAIN TAPROOT"

The principle that we shall find no enduring strength until we first admit complete defeat is the main taproot from which our whole Society has sprung and flowered.
TWELVE STEPS AND TWELVE TRADITIONS, pp. 21-22

Defeated, and knowing it, I arrived at the doors of A.A., alone and afraid of the unknown. A power outside of myself had picked me up off my bed, guided me to the phone book, then to the bus stop, and through the doors of Alcoholics Anonymous. Once inside A.A. I experienced a sense of being loved and accepted, something I had not felt since early childhood. May I never lose the sense of wonder I experienced on that first evening with A.A., the greatest event of my entire life.

SOLACE FOR CONFUSION

Obviously, the dilemma of the wanderer from faith is that of profound confusion. He thinks himself lost to the comfort of any conviction at all. He cannot attain in even a small degree the assurance of the believer, the agnostic, or the atheist. He is the bewildered one.

TWELVE STEPS AND TWELVE TRADITIONS, p. 28

The concept of God was one that I struggled with during my early years of sobriety. The images that came to me, conjured from my past, were heavy with fear, rejection and condemnation. Then I heard my friend Ed's image of a Higher Power: As a boy he had been allowed a litter of puppies, provided that he assume responsibility for their care. Each morning he would find the unavoidable "by-products" of the puppies on the kitchen floor. Despite frustration, Ed said he couldn't get angry because "that's the nature of puppies." Ed felt that God viewed our defects and shortcomings with a similar understanding and warmth. I've often found solace from my personal confusion in Ed's calming concept of God.

NOTHING GROWS IN THE DARK

We will want the good that is in us all, even in the worst of us, to flower and to grow.

AS BILL SEES IT, p. 10

With the self-discipline and insight gained from practicing Step Ten, I begin to know the gratifications of sobriety—not as mere abstinence from alcohol, but as recovery in every department of my life.

I renew hope, regenerate faith, and regain the dignity of self-respect. I discover the word "and" in the phrase "and when we were wrong, promptly admitted it."

Reassured that I am no longer always wrong, I learn to accept myself as I am, with a new sense of the miracles of sobriety and serenity.

TRUE TOLERANCE

Finally, we begin to see that all people, including ourselves, are to some extent emotionally ill as well as frequently wrong, and then we approach true tolerance and see what real love for our fellows actually means.

TWELVE STEPS AND TWELVE TRADITIONS, p. 92

The thought occurred to me that all people are emotionally ill to some extent. How could we not be? Who among us is spiritually perfect? Who among us is physically perfect? How could any of us be emotionally perfect? Therefore, what else are we to do but bear with one another and treat each other as we would be treated in similar circumstances? That is what love really is.

WHAT WE KNOW BEST

"Shoemaker, stick to thy last!" . . . *better do one thing supremely well than many badly. That is the central theme of this Tradition [Five]. Around it our Society gathers in unity. The very life of our Fellowship requires the preservation of this principle.*
TWELVE STEPS AND TWELVE TRADITIONS, p. 150

The survival of A.A. depends upon unity. What would happen if a group decided to become an employment agency, a treatment center or a social service agency? Too much specialization leads to no specialization, to frittering of efforts and, finally, to decline. I have the qualifications to share my sufferings and my way of recovery with the newcomer. Conformity to A.A.'s primary purpose insures the safety of the wonderful gift of sobriety, so my responsibility is enormous. The life of millions of alcoholics is closely tied to my competence in "carrying the message to the still-suffering alcoholic."

"BY FAITH AND BY WORKS"

On anvils of experience, the structure of our Society was hammered out. . . . Thus has it been with A.A. By faith and by works we have been able to build upon the lessons of an incredible experience. They live today in the Twelve Traditions of Alcoholics Anonymous, which—God willing—shall sustain us in unity for so long as He may need us.

TWELVE STEPS AND TWELVE TRADITIONS, p. 131

God has allowed me the right to be wrong in order for our Fellowship to exist as it does today. If I place God's will first in my life, it is very likely that A.A. as I know it today will remain as it is.

A.A.'s HEARTBEAT

Without unity, the heart of A.A. would cease to beat; . . .

AS BILL SEES IT, p. 125

Without unity I would be unable to recover in A.A. on a daily basis. By practicing unity within my group, with other A.A. members and at all levels of this great Fellowship, I receive a pronounced feeling of knowing that I am a part of a miracle that was divinely inspired. The ability of Bill W. and Dr. Bob, working together and passing it on to other members, tells me that to give it away is to keep it. Unity is oneness and yet the whole Fellowship is for all of us.

ONE ULTIMATE AUTHORITY

For our group purpose there is but one ultimate authority—a loving God as He may express Himself in our group conscience.

TWELVE STEPS AND TWELVE TRADITIONS, p. 132

When I am chosen to carry some small responsibility for my fellows, I ask that God grant me the patience, open-mindedness, and willingness to listen to those I would lead. I must remind myself that I am the trusted servant of others, not their "governor," "teacher," or "instructor." God guides my words and my actions, and my responsibility is to heed His suggestions. Trust is my watchword, I trust others who lead. In the Fellowship of A.A., I entrust God with the ultimate authority of "running the show."

GLOBAL SHARING

The only thing that matters is that he is an alcoholic who has found a key to sobriety. These legacies of suffering and of recovery are easily passed among alcoholics, one to the other. This is our gift from God, and its bestowal upon others like us is the one aim that today animates A.A.'s all around the globe.
TWELVE STEPS AND TWELVE TRADITIONS, p. 151

The strength of Alcoholics Anonymous lies in the desire of each member and of each group around the world to share with other alcoholics their suffering and the steps taken to gain, and maintain, recovery. By keeping a conscious contact with my Higher Power, I make sure that I always nurture my desire to help other alcoholics, thus insuring the continuity of the wonderful fraternity of Alcoholics Anonymous.

AN UNBROKEN TRADITION

We conceive the survival and spread of Alcoholics Anonymous to be something of far greater importance than the weight we could collectively throw back of any other cause.
TWELVE STEPS AND TWELVE TRADITIONS, p. 177

How much it means to me that an unbroken tradition of more than half a century is a thread that connects me to Bill W. and Dr. Bob. How much more grounded I feel to be in a Fellowship whose aims are constant and unflagging. I am grateful that the energies of A.A. have never been scattered, but focused instead on our members and on individual sobriety.

My beliefs are what make me human; I am free to hold any opinion, but A.A.'s purpose—so clearly stated fifty years ago—is for me to keep sober. That purpose has promoted round-the-clock meeting schedules, and the thousands of intergroup and central service offices, with their thousands of volunteers. Like the sun focused through a magnifying glass, A.A.'s single vision has lit a fire of faith in sobriety in millions of hearts, including mine.

OUR SURVIVAL

Since recovery from alcoholism is life itself to us, it is imperative that we preserve in full strength our means of survival.

TWELVE STEPS AND TWELVE TRADITIONS, p. 177

The *honesty* expressed by the members of A.A. in meetings has the power to open my mind. Nothing can block the flow of energy that *honesty* carries with it. The only obstacle to this flow of energy is inebriation, but even then, no one will find a closed door if he or she has left and chooses to return. Once he or she has received the gift of sobriety, each A.A. member is challenged on a daily basis to accept a program of *honesty*.

My Higher Power created me for a purpose in life. I ask him to accept my honest efforts to continue on my journey in the spiritual way of life. I call on Him for strength to know and seek His will.

LIVE AND LET LIVE

Never since it began has Alcoholics Anonymous been divided by a major controversial issue. Nor has our Fellowship ever publicly taken sides on any question in an embattled world. This, however, has been no earned virtue. It could almost be said that we were born with it. . . . "So long as we don't argue these matters privately, it's a cinch we never shall publicly."

TWELVE STEPS AND TWELVE TRADITIONS, p. 176

Do I remember that I have a right to my opinion but that others don't have to share it? That's the spirit of "Live and Let Live." The Serenity Prayer reminds me, with God's help, to "Accept the things I cannot change." Am I still trying to change others? When it comes to "Courage to change the things I can," do I remember that my opinions are mine, and yours are yours? Am I still afraid to be me? When it comes to "Wisdom to know the difference," do I remember that my opinions come from *my* experience? If I have a know-it-all attitude, aren't I being deliberately controversial?

AVOIDING CONTROVERSY

All history affords us the spectacle of striving nations and groups finally torn asunder because they were designed for, or tempted into, controversy. Others fell apart because of sheer self-righteousness while trying to enforce upon the rest of mankind some millennium of their own specification.

TWELVE STEPS AND TWELVE TRADITIONS, p. 176

As an A.A. member and sponsor, I know I can cause real damage if I yield to temptation and give opinions and advice on another's medical, marital, or religious problems. I am not a doctor, counselor, or lawyer. I cannot tell anyone how he or she should live; however, I can share how I came through similar situations without drinking, and how A.A.'s Steps and Traditions help me in dealing with my life.

I CANNOT CHANGE THE WIND

It is easy to let up on the spiritual program of action and rest on our laurels. We are headed for trouble if we do, for alcohol is a subtle foe.

ALCOHOLICS ANONYMOUS, p. 85

My first sponsor told me there were two things to say about prayer and meditation: first, I had to start and second, I had to continue. When I came to A.A. my spiritual life was bankrupt; if I considered God at all, He was to be called upon only when my self-will was incapable of a task or when over-whelming fears had eroded my ego.

Today I am grateful for a new life, one in which my prayers are those of thanksgiving. My prayer time is more for listening than for talking. I know today that if I cannot change the wind, I can adjust my sail. I know the difference between superstition and spirituality. I know there is a graceful way of being right, and many ways to be wrong.

KEEPING OPTIMISM AFLOAT

The other Steps can keep most of us sober and some-how functioning. But Step Eleven can keep us grow-ing, . . .

THE LANGUAGE OF THE HEART, p. 240

A sober alcoholic finds it much easier to be optimis-tic about life. Optimism is the natural result of my finding myself gradually able to make the best, rather than the worst, of each situation. As my physical sobriety continues, I come out of the fog, gain a clearer perspective and am better able to de-termine what courses of action to take. As vital as physical sobriety is, I can achieve a greater poten-tial for myself by developing an ever-increasing willingness to avail myself of the guidance and di-rection of a Higher Power. My ability to do so comes from my learning—and practicing—the principles of the A.A. program. The melding of my physical and spiritual sobriety produces the sub-stance of a more positive life.

FOCUSING AND LISTENING

There is a direct linkage among self-examination, meditation, and prayer. Taken separately, these practices can bring much relief and benefit.
 TWELVE STEPS AND TWELVE TRADITIONS, p. 98

If I do my self-examination first, then surely, I'll have enough humility to pray and meditate—because I'll see and feel my need for them. Some wish to begin and end with prayer, leaving the self-examination and meditation to take place in between, whereas others start with meditation, listening for advice from God about their still hidden or unacknowledged defects. Still others engage in written and verbal work on their defects, ending with a prayer of praise and thanksgiving. These three— self-examination, meditation and prayer—form a circle, without a beginning or an end. No matter where, or how, I start, I eventually arrive at my destination: a better life.

A DAILY DISCIPLINE

. . . when they [self-examination, meditation and prayer] are logically related and interwoven, the result is an unshakable foundation for life.
TWELVE STEPS AND TWELVE TRADITIONS, p. 98

The last three Steps of the program invoke God's loving discipline upon my willful nature. If I devote just a few moments every night to a review of the highlights of my day, along with an acknowledgement of those aspects that didn't please me so much, I gain a personal history of myself, one that is essential to my journey into self-discovery. I was able to note my growth, or lack of it, and to ask in prayerful meditation to be relieved of those continuing shortcomings that cause me pain. Meditation and prayer also teach me the art of focusing and listening. I find that the turmoil of the day gets tuned out as I pray for His will and guidance. The practice of asking Him to help me in my strivings for perfection puts a new slant on the tedium of any day, because I know there is honor in any job done well. The daily discipline of prayer and meditation will keep me in fit spiritual condition, able to face whatever the day brings—without the thought of a drink.

"THE QUALITY OF FAITH"

*This . . . has to do with the quality of faith.
. . . In no deep or meaningful sense had we ever
taken stock of ourselves. . . . We had not even
prayed rightly. We had always said, "Grant me my
wishes" instead of "Thy will be done."*

TWELVE STEPS AND TWELVE TRADITIONS, p. 32

God does not grant me material possessions, take
away my suffering, or spare me from disasters, but
He does give me a good life, the ability to cope, and
peace of mind. My prayers are simple: first, they
express my gratitude for the good things in my life,
regardless of how hard I have to search for them;
and second, I ask only for the strength and the wisdom to do His will. He answers with solutions to
my problems, sustaining my ability to live through
daily frustrations with a serenity I did not believe
existed, and with the strength to practice the principles of A.A. in all of my everyday affairs.

GOING WITH THE FLOW

Sought through prayer and meditation to improve our conscious contact with God as we understood Him. . . .

TWELVE STEPS AND TWELVE TRADITIONS, p. 96

The first words I speak when arising in the morning are, "I arise, O God, to do Thy will." This is the shortest prayer I know and it is deeply ingrained in me. Prayer doesn't change God's attitude toward me; it changes my attitude toward God. As distinguished from prayer, meditation is a quiet time, without words. To be centered is to be physically relaxed, emotionally calm, mentally focused and spiritually aware.

One way to keep the channel open and to improve my conscious contact with God is to maintain a grateful attitude. On the days when I am grateful, good things seem to happen in my life. The instant I start cursing things in my life, however, the flow of good stops. God did not interrupt the flow; my own negativity did.

LET GO AND LET GOD

. . . praying only for knowledge of His will for us and the power to carry that out.

TWELVE STEPS AND TWELVE TRADITIONS, p. 96

When I "Let Go and Let God," I think more clearly and wisely. Without having to think about it, I quickly let go of things that cause me immediate pain and discomfort. Because I find it hard to let go of the kind of worrisome thoughts and attitudes that cause me immense anguish, all I need do during those times is allow God, as I understand Him, to release them for me, and then and there, I let go of the thoughts, memories and attitudes that are troubling me.

When I receive help from God, as I understand Him, I can live my life one day at a time and handle whatever challenges that come my way. Only then can I live a life of victory over alcohol, in comfortable sobriety.

AN INDIVIDUAL ADVENTURE

Meditation is something which can always be further developed. It has no boundaries, either of width or height. Aided by such instruction and example as we can find, it is essentially an individual adventure, something which each one of us works out in his own way.

TWELVE STEPS AND TWELVE TRADITIONS, p. 101

My spiritual growth is with God as I understand Him. With Him I find my true inner self. Daily meditation and prayer strengthen and renew my source of well-being. I receive then the openness to accept all that He has to offer. With God I have the reassurance that my journey will be as He wants for me, and for that I am grateful to have God in my life.

STEPPING INTO THE SUNLIGHT

But first of all we shall want sunlight; nothing much can grow in the dark. Meditation is our step out into the sun.

AS BILL SEES IT, p. 10

Sometimes I think I don't have time for prayer and meditation, forgetting that I always found the time to drink. It is possible to make time for anything I want to do if I want it badly enough. When I start the routine of prayer and meditation, it's a good idea to plan to devote a small amount of time to it. I read a page from our Fellowship's books in the morning, and say "Thank You, God," when I go to bed at night. As prayer becomes a habit, I will increase the time spent on it, without even noticing the foray it makes into my busy day. If I have trouble praying, I just repeat the Lord's Prayer because it really covers everything. Then I think of what I can be grateful for and say a word of thanks.

I don't need to shut myself in a closet to pray. It can be done even in a room full of people. I just remove myself mentally for an instant. As the practice of prayer continues, I will find I don't need words, for God can, and does, hear my thoughts through silence.

A SENSE OF BELONGING

Perhaps one of the greatest rewards of meditation and prayer is the sense of belonging *that comes to us.*

TWELVE STEPS AND TWELVE TRADITIONS, p. 105

That's what it is—belonging! After a session of meditation I knew that the feeling I was experiencing was a sense of belonging because I was so relaxed. I felt quieter inside, more willing to discard little irritations. I appreciated my sense of humor. What I also experience in my daily practice is the sheer pleasure of belonging to the creative flow of God's world. How propitious for us that prayer and meditation are written right into our A.A. way of life.

SELF-ACCEPTANCE

We know that God lovingly watches over us. We know that when we turn to Him, all will be well with us, here and hereafter.
TWELVE STEPS AND TWELVE TRADITIONS, p. 105

I pray for the willingness to remember that I am a child of God, a divine soul in human form, and that my most basic and urgent life-task is to accept, know, love and nurture myself. As I accept myself, I am accepting God's will. As I know and love myself, I am knowing and loving God. As I nurture myself I am acting on God's guidance.

I pray for the willingness to let go of my arrogant self-criticism, and to praise God by humbly accepting and caring for myself.

MORNING THOUGHTS

Ask Him in your morning meditation what you can do each day for the man who is still sick.

ALCOHOLICS ANONYMOUS, p. 164

For many years I pondered over God's will for me, believing that perhaps a great destiny had been ordained for my life. After all, having been born into a specific faith, hadn't I been told early that I was "chosen"? It *finally* occurred to me, as I considered the above passage, that God's will for me was simply that I practice Step Twelve on a daily basis. Furthermore, I realized I should do this to the best of my ability. I soon learned that the practice aids me in keeping my life in the context of the day at hand.

LOOKING OUTWARD

We ask especially for freedom from self-will, and are careful to make no requests for ourselves only. We may ask for ourselves, however, if others will be helped. We are careful never to pray for our own selfish ends.

ALCOHOLICS ANONYMOUS, p. 87

As an active alcoholic, I allowed selfishness to run rampant in my life. I was so attached to my drinking and other selfish habits that people and moral principles came second. Now, when I pray for the good of others rather than my "own selfish ends," I practice a discipline in letting go of selfish attachments, caring for my fellows and preparing for the day when I will be required to let go of all earthly attachments.

INTUITION AND INSPIRATION

. . . we ask God for inspiration, an intuitive thought or a decision. We relax and take it easy. We don't struggle.

ALCOHOLICS ANONYMOUS, p. 86

I invest my time in what I truly love. Step Eleven is a discipline that allows me and my Higher Power to be together, reminding me that, with God's help, intuition and inspiration are possible. Practice of the Step brings on self-love. In a consistent attempt to improve my conscious contact with a Higher Power, I am subtly reminded of my unhealthy past, with its patterns of grandiose thinking and false feelings of omnipotence. When I ask for the power to carry out God's will for me, I am made aware of my powerlessness. Humility and a healthy self-love are compatible, a direct result of working Step Eleven.

VITAL SUSTENANCE

Those of us who have come to make regular use of prayer would no more do without it than we would refuse air, food, or sunshine. And for the same reason. When we refuse air, light, or food, the body suffers. And when we turn away from meditation and prayer, we likewise deprive our minds, our emotions, and our intuitions of vitally needed support.
TWELVE STEPS AND TWELVE TRADITIONS, p. 97

Step Eleven doesn't have to overwhelm me. Conscious contact with God can be as simple, and as profound, as conscious contact with another human being. I can smile. I can listen. I can forgive. Every encounter with another is an opportunity for prayer, for acknowledging God's presence within me.

Today I can bring myself a little closer to my Higher Power. The more I choose to seek the beauty of God's work in other people, the more certain of His presence I will become.

A DAILY REPRIEVE

What we really have is a daily reprieve contingent on the maintenance of our spiritual condition.
ALCOHOLICS ANONYMOUS, p. 85

Maintaining my spiritual condition is like working out every day, planning for the marathon, swimming laps, jogging. It's staying in good shape spiritually, and that requires prayer and meditation. The single most important way for me to improve my conscious contact with a Higher Power is to pray and meditate. I am as powerless over alcohol as I am to turn back the waves of the sea; no human force had the power to overcome my alcoholism. Now I am able to breathe the air of joy, happiness and wisdom. I have the power to love and react to events around me with the eyes of a faith in things that are not readily apparent. My daily reprieve means that, no matter how difficult or painful things appear today, I can draw on the power of the program to stay liberated from my cunning, baffling and powerful illness.

OVERCOMING LONELINESS

Almost without exception, alcoholics are tortured by loneliness. Even before our drinking got bad and people began to cut us off, nearly all of us suffered the feeling that we didn't quite belong.

AS BILL SEES IT, p. 90

The agonies and the void that I often felt inside occur less and less frequently in my life today. I have learned to cope with solitude. It is only when I am alone and calm that I am able to communicate with God, for He cannot reach me when I am in turmoil. It is good to maintain contact with God at all times, but it is absolutely essential that, when everything seems to go wrong, I maintain that contact through prayer and meditation.

A SAFETY NET

Occasionally. . . . We are seized with a rebellion so sickening that we simply won't pray. When these things happen we should not think too ill of ourselves. We should simply resume prayer as soon as we can, doing what we know to be good for us.
TWELVE STEPS AND TWELVE TRADITIONS, p. 105

Sometimes I scream, stomp my feet, and turn my back on my Higher Power. Then my disease tells me that I am a failure, and that if I stay angry I'll surely get drunk. In those moments of self-will it's as if I've slipped over a cliff and am hanging by one hand. The above passage is my safety net, in that it urges me to try some new behavior, such as being kind and patient with myself. It assures me that my Higher Power will wait until I am willing once again to risk letting go, to land in the net, and to pray.

"I WAS SLIPPING FAST"

We A.A.'s are active folk, enjoying the satisfactions of dealing with the realities of life, . . . So it isn't surprising that we often tend to slight serious meditation and prayer as something not really necessary.
TWELVE STEPS AND TWELVE TRADITIONS, p. 96

I had been slipping away from the program for some time, but it took a death threat from a terminal disease to bring me back, and particularly to the practice of the Eleventh Step of our blessed Fellowship. Although I had fifteen years of sobriety and was still very active in the program, I knew that the quality of my sobriety had slipped badly. Eighteen months later, a checkup revealed a malignant tumor and a prognosis of certain death within six months. Despair settled in when I enrolled in a rehab program, after which I suffered two small strokes which revealed two large brain tumors. As I kept hitting new bottoms I had to ask myself why this was happening to me. God allowed me to recognize my dishonesty and to become teachable again. Miracles began to happen. But primarily I relearned the whole meaning of the Eleventh Step. My physical condition has improved dramatically, but my illness is minor compared to what I almost lost completely.

"THY WILL, NOT MINE"

. . . when making specific requests, it will be well to add to each one of them this qualification. ". . . if it be Thy will."
TWELVE STEPS AND TWELVE TRADITIONS, p.102

I ask simply that throughout the day God place in me the best understanding of His will that I can have for that day, and that I be given the grace by which I may carry it out. As the day goes on, I can pause when facing situations that must be met and decisions that must be made, and renew the simple request: "Thy will, not mine, be done."

I must always keep in mind that in every situation I am responsible for the effort and God is responsible for the outcome. I can "Let Go and Let God" by humbly repeating: "Thy will, not mine, be done." Patience and persistence in seeking His will for me will free me from the pain of selfish expectations.

A CLASSIC PRAYER

Lord, make me a channel for thy peace—that where there is hatred, I may bring love—that where there is wrong, I may bring the spirit of forgiveness—that where there is discord, I may bring harmony—that where there is error, I may bring truth—that where there is doubt, I may bring faith—that where there is despair, I may bring hope—that where there are shadows, I may bring light—that where there is sadness, I may bring joy. Lord, grant that I may seek rather to comfort than to be comforted—to understand, than to be understood—to love, than to be loved. For it is by self-forgetting that one finds. It is by forgiving that one is forgiven. It is by dying that one awakens to Eternal Life. Amen.

TWELVE STEPS AND TWELVE TRADITIONS, p. 99

No matter where I am in my spiritual growth, the St. Francis prayer helps me improve my conscious contact with the God of my understanding. I think that one of the great advantages of my faith in God is that I do not understand Him, or Her, or It. It may be that my relationship with my Higher Power is so fruitful that I do not have to understand. All that I am certain of is that if I work the Eleventh Step regularly, as best I can, I will continue to improve my conscious contact, I will know His will for me, and I will have the power to carry it out.

ONLY TWO SINS

. . . there are only two sins; the first is to interfere with the growth of another human being, and the second is to interfere with one's own growth.
ALCOHOLICS ANONYMOUS, p. 542

Happiness is such an elusive state. How often do my "prayers" for others involve "hidden" prayers for my own agenda? How often is my search for happiness a boulder in the path of growth for another, or even myself? Seeking growth through humility and acceptance brings things that appear to be anything but good, wholesome and vital. Yet in looking back, I can see that pain, struggles and setbacks have all contributed eventually to serenity through growth in the program.

I ask my Higher Power to help me not cause another's lack of growth today—or my own.

"HOLD YOUR FACE TO THE LIGHT"

Believe more deeply. Hold your face up to the Light,
even though for the moment you do not see.

AS BILL SEES IT, p. 3

One Sunday in October, during my morning meditation, I glanced out the window at the ash tree in our front yard. At once I was overwhelmed by its magnificent, golden color! As I stared in awe at God's work of art, the leaves began to fall and, within minutes, the branches were bare. Sadness came over me as I thought of the winter months ahead, but just as I was reflecting on autumn's annual process, God's message came through. Like the trees, stripped of their leaves in the fall, sprout new blossoms in the spring, I had had my compulsive, selfish ways removed by God in order for me to blossom into a sober, joyful member of A.A. Thank you, God, for the changing seasons and for my ever-changing life.

A UNIVERSAL SEARCH

*Be quick to see where religious people are right.
Make use of what they offer.*
ALCOHOLICS ANONYMOUS, p. 87

I do not claim to have all the answers in spiritual matters, any more than I claim to have all the answers about alcoholism. There are others who are also engaged in a spiritual search. If I keep an open mind about what others have to say, I have much to gain. My sobriety is greatly enriched, and my practice of the Eleventh Step more fruitful, when I use both the literature and practices of my Judeo-Christian tradition, and the resources of other religions. Thus, I receive support from many sources in staying away from the first drink.

A POWERFUL TRADITION

In the years before the publication of the book, "Alcoholics Anonymous," we had no name. . . . By a narrow majority the verdict was for naming our book "The Way Out." . . . One of our early lone members . . . found exactly twelve books already titled "The Way Out." . . . So "Alcoholics Anonymous" became first choice. That's how we got a name for our book of experience, a name for our movement and, as we are now beginning to see, a tradition of the greatest spiritual import.

"A.A. TRADITION: HOW IT DEVELOPED," pp. 35-36

Beginning with Bill's momentous decision in Akron to make a telephone call rather than a visit to the hotel bar, how often has a Higher Power made itself felt at crucial moments in our history! The eventual importance that the principle of anonymity would acquire was but dimly perceived, if at all, in those early days. There seems to have been an element of chance even in the choice of a name for our Fellowship.

God is no stranger to anonymity and often appears in human affairs in the guises of "luck," "chance," or "coincidence." If anonymity, somewhat fortuitously, became the spiritual basis for all of our Traditions, perhaps God was acting anonymously on our behalf.

THE HAZARDS OF PUBLICITY

People who symbolize causes and ideas fill a deep human need. We of A.A. do not question that. But we do have to soberly face the fact that being in the public eye is hazardous, especially for us.
TWELVE STEPS AND TWELVE TRADITIONS, p. 181

As a recovered alcoholic I must make an effort to put into practice the principles of the A.A. program, which are founded on honesty, truth and humility. While I was drinking I was constantly trying to be in the limelight. Now that I am conscious of my mistakes and of my former lack of integrity, it would not be honest to seek prestige, even for the justifiable purpose of promoting the A.A. message of recovery. Is the publicity that centers around the A.A. Fellowship and the miracles it produces not worth much more? Why not let the people around us appreciate by themselves the changes that A.A. has brought in us, for that will be a far better recommendation for the Fellowship than any I could make.

THE PERILS OF THE LIMELIGHT

In the beginning, the press could not understand our refusal of all personal publicity. They were genuinely baffled by our insistence upon anonymity. Then they got the point. Here was something rare in the world —a society which said it wished to publicize its principles and its work, but not its individual members. The press was delighted with this attitude. Ever since, these friends have reported A.A. with an enthusiasm which the most ardent members would find hard to match.

TWELVE STEPS AND TWELVE TRADITIONS, p. 182

It is essential for my personal survival and that of the Fellowship that I not use A.A. to put myself in the limelight. Anonymity is a way for me to work on my humility. Since pride is one of my most dangerous shortcomings, practicing humility is one of the best ways to overcome it. The Fellowship of A.A. gains worldwide recognition by its various methods of publicizing its principles and its work, not by its individual members advertising themselves. The attraction created by my changing attitudes and my altruism contributes much more to the welfare of A.A. than self-promotion.

ATTRACTION, NOT PROMOTION

Through many painful experiences, we think we have arrived at what that policy ought to be. It is the opposite in many ways of usual promotional practice. We found that we had to rely upon the principle of attraction *rather than of promotion.*
TWELVE STEPS AND TWELVE TRADITIONS, pp. 180–81

While I was drinking I reacted with anger, self-pity and defiance against anyone who wanted to change me. All I wanted then was to be accepted by another human simply as I was and, curiously, that is what I found in A.A. I became the custodian of this concept of attraction, which is the principle of our Fellowship's public relations. It is by attraction that I can best reach the alcoholic who still suffers.

I thank God for having given me the attraction of a well-planned and established program of Steps and Traditions. Through humility and the support of my fellow sober members, I have been able to practice the A.A. way of life through attraction, not promotion.

"ACTIVE GUARDIANS"

To us, however, it represents far more than a sound public relations policy. It is more than a denial of self-seeking. This Tradition is a constant and practical reminder that personal ambition has no place in A.A. In it, each member becomes an active guardian of our Fellowship.

TWELVE STEPS AND TWELVE TRADITIONS, p. 183

The basic concept of humility is expressed in the Eleventh Tradition: it allows me to participate completely in the program in such a simple, yet profound, manner; it fulfills my need to be an integral part of a significant whole. Humility brings me closer to the actual spirit of togetherness and oneness, without which I could not stay sober. In remembering that every member is an example of sobriety, each one living the Eleventh Tradition, I am able to experience freedom because each one of us is anonymous.

PROTECTION FOR ALL

At the personal level, anonymity provides protection for all members from identification as alcoholics, a safeguard often of special importance to newcomers. At the level of press, radio, TV, and films, anonymity stresses the equality in the Fellowship of all members by putting the brake on those who might otherwise exploit their A.A. affiliation to achieve recognition, power, or personal gain.

"UNDERSTANDING ANONYMITY," p. 5

Attraction is the main force in the Fellowship of A.A. The miracle of continuous sobriety of alcoholics within A.A. confirms this fact every day. It would be harmful if the Fellowship promoted itself by publicizing, through the media of radio and TV, the sobriety of well-known public personalities who became members of A.A. If these personalities happened to have slips, outsiders would think our movement is not strong and they might question the veracity of the miracle of the century. Alcoholics Anonymous is not anonymous, but its members should be.

"SUGGESTED" STEPS

Our Twelfth Step also says that as a result of practicing all the Steps, we have each found something called a spiritual awakening. . . . A.A.'s manner of making ready to receive this gift lies in the practice of the Twelve Steps in our program."
TWELVE STEPS AND TWELVE TRADITIONS, pp. 106-07

I remember my sponsor's answer when I told him that the Steps were "suggested." He replied that they are "suggested" in the same way that, if you were to jump out of an airplane with a parachute, it is "suggested" that you pull the ripcord to save your life. He pointed out that it was "suggested" I practice the Twelve Steps, if I wanted to save my life. So I try to remember daily that I have a whole program of recovery based on all Twelve of the "suggested" Steps.

SERENITY

Having had a spiritual awakening as the result of these steps, . . .

TWELVE STEPS AND TWELVE TRADITIONS, p. 106

As I continued to go to meetings and work the Steps, something began to happen to me. I felt confused because I wasn't sure what it was that I was feeling, and then I realized I was experiencing serenity. It was a good feeling, but where had it come from? Then I realized it had come ". . . as the result of these steps." The program may not always be easy to practice, but I had to acknowledge that my serenity had come to me after working the Steps. As I work the Steps in everything I do, practicing these principles in all my affairs, now I find that I am awake to God, to others, and to myself. The spiritual awakening I have enjoyed as the result of working the Steps is the awareness that I am no longer alone.

IN ALL OUR AFFAIRS

*. . . we tried to carry this message to alcoholics, and
to practice these principles in all our affairs.*
TWELVE STEPS AND TWELVE TRADITIONS, p. 106

I find that carrying the message of recovery to other
alcoholics is easy because it helps me to stay sober
and it provides me with a sense of well-being about
my own recovery. The hard part is *practicing these
principles in all my affairs.* It is important that I
share the benefits I receive from A.A., especially at
home. Doesn't my family deserve the same patience, tolerance and understanding I so readily
give to the alcoholic? When reviewing my day I try
to ask, "Did I have a chance to be a friend today
and miss it?" "Did I have a chance to rise above a
nasty situation and avoid it?" "Did I have a chance
to say 'I'm sorry,' and refuse to?"

Just as I ask God for help with my alcoholism
each day, I ask for help in extending my recovery to
include all situations and *all* people!

INTO ACTION

A.A. is more than a set of principles; it is a society of alcoholics in action. We must carry the message, else we ourselves can wither and those who haven't been given the truth may die.

AS BILL SEES IT, p. 13

I desperately wanted to live, but if I was to succeed, I had to become active in our God-given program. I joined what became my group, where I opened the hall, made coffee, and cleaned up. I had been sober about three months when an oldtimer told me I was doing Twelfth-Step work. What a satisfying realization that was! I felt I was really accomplishing something. God had given me a second chance, A.A. had shown me the way, and these gifts were not only free—they were also priceless! Now the joy of seeing newcomers grow reminds me of where I have come from, where I am now, and the limitless possibilities that lie ahead. I need to attend meetings because they recharge my batteries so that I have light when it's needed. I'm still a beginner in service work, but already I am receiving more than I'm giving. I can't keep it unless I give it away. *I am responsible when another reaches out for help.* I want to be there—sober.

A NEW STATE OF CONSCIOUSNESS

He has been granted a gift which amounts to a new state of consciousness and being.
TWELVE STEPS AND TWELVE TRADITIONS, p. 107

Many of us in A.A. puzzle over what is a spiritual awakening. I tended to look for a miracle, something dramatic and earth-shattering. But what usually happens is that a sense of well-being, a feeling of peace, transforms us into a new level of awareness. That's what happened to me. My insanity and inner turmoil disappeared and I entered into a new dimension of hope, love and peace. I think the degree to which I continue to experience this new dimension is in direct proportion to the sincerity, depth and devotion with which I practice the Twelve Steps of A.A.

WHEN THE CHIPS ARE DOWN

When we developed still more, we discovered the best possible source of emotional stability to be God Himself. We found that dependence upon His perfect justice, forgiveness, and love was healthy, and that it would work where nothing else would. If we really depended upon God, we couldn't very well play God to our fellows nor would we feel the urge wholly to rely on human protection and care.
TWELVE STEPS AND TWELVE TRADITIONS, p. 116

It has been my experience that, when all human resources appear to have failed, there is always One who will never desert me. Moreover, He is always there to share my joy, to steer me down the right path, and to confide in when no one else will do. While my well-being and happiness can be added to, or diminished, by human efforts, only God can provide the loving nourishment upon which I depend for my daily spiritual health.

TRUE AMBITION

True ambition is not what we thought it was. True ambition is the deep desire to live usefully and walk humbly under the grace of God.
TWELVE STEPS AND TWELVE TRADITIONS, pp. 124-25

During my drinking years, my one and only concern was to have my fellow man think highly of me. My ambition in everything I did was to have the power to be at the top. My inner self kept telling me something else but I couldn't accept it. I didn't even allow myself to realize that I wore a mask continually. Finally, when the mask came off and I cried out to the only God I could conceive, the Fellowship of A.A., my group and the Twelve Steps were there. I learned how to change resentments into acceptance, fear into hope and anger into love. I have learned also, through loving without undo expectations, through sharing my concerns and caring for my fellow man, that each day can be joyous and fruitful. I begin and end my day with thanks to God, who has so generously shed His grace on me.

SERVICE

Life will take on new meaning. To watch people recover, to see them help others, to watch loneliness vanish, to see a fellowship grow up about you, to have a host of friends—this is an experience you must not miss. . . . Frequent contact with newcomers and with each other is the bright spot of our lives.

ALCOHOLICS ANONYMOUS, p. 89

It is through service that the greatest rewards are to be found. But to be in a position of offering true, useful and effective service to others, I must first work on myself. This means that I have to abandon myself to God, admitting my faults and clearing away the wreckage of my past. Work on myself has taught me how to find the necessary peace and serenity to successfully merge inspiration and experience. I have learned how to be, in the truest sense, an open channel of sobriety.

LOVE WITH NO PRICE TAG

When the Twelfth Step is seen in its full implication, it is really talking about the kind of love that has no price tag on it.
TWELVE STEPS AND TWELVE TRADITIONS, p. 106

In order for me to start working the Twelfth Step, I had to work on sincerity, honesty, and to learn to act with humility. Carrying the message is a gift of myself, no matter how many years of sobriety I may have accumulated. My dreams can become reality. I solidify my sobriety by sharing what I have received freely. As I look back to that time when I began my recovery, there was already a seed of hope that I could help another drunk pull himself out of his alcoholic mire. My wish to help another drunk is the key to my spiritual health. But I never forget that God acts through me. I am only His instrument.

Even if the other person is not ready, there is success, because my effort in his behalf has helped me to remain sober and to become stronger. To act, to never grow weary in my Twelfth Step work, is the key. If I am capable of laughing today, let me not forget those days when I cried. God reminds me that I can feel compassion!

CARRYING THE MESSAGE

Now, what about the rest of the Twelfth Step? The wonderful energy it releases and the eager action by which it carries our message to the next suffering alcoholic and which finally translates the Twelve Steps into action upon all our affairs is the payoff, the magnificent reality, of Alcoholics Anonymous.

TWELVE STEPS AND TWELVE TRADITIONS, p. 109

To renounce the alcoholic world is not to abandon it, but to act upon principles I have come to love and cherish, and to restore in others who still suffer the serenity I have come to know. When I am truly committed to this purpose, it matters little what clothes I wear or how I make a living. My task is to carry the message, and to lead by example, not design.

"A GENUINE HUMILITY"

. . . we are actually to practice a genuine humility. This is to the end that our great blessings may never spoil us; that we shall forever live in thankful contemplation of Him who presides over us all.
TWELVE STEPS AND TWELVE TRADITIONS, p. 192

Experience has taught me that my alcoholic personality tends to be grandiose. While having seemingly good intentions, I can go off on tangents in pursuit of my "causes." My ego takes over and I lose sight of my primary purpose. I may even take credit for God's handiwork in my life. Such an overstated feeling of my own importance is dangerous to my sobriety and could cause great harm to A.A. as a whole.

My safeguard, the Twelfth Tradition, serves to keep me humble. I realize, both as an individual and as a member of the Fellowship, that I cannot boast of my accomplishments, and that "God is doing for us what we could not do for ourselves."

A COMMON SOLUTION

The tremendous fact for every one of us is that we have discovered a common solution. We have a way out on which we can absolutely agree, and upon which we can join in brotherly and harmonious action. This is the great news this book carries to those who suffer from alcoholism.

ALCOHOLICS ANONYMOUS, p. 17

The most far-reaching Twelfth Step work was the publication of our Big Book, *Alcoholics Anonymous.* Few can equal that book for carrying the message. My idea is to get out of myself and simply do what I can. Even if I haven't been asked to sponsor and my phone rarely rings, I am still able to do Twelfth Step work. I get involved in "brotherly and harmonious action." At meetings I show up early to greet people and to help set up, and to share my experience, strength and hope. I also do what I can with service work. My Higher Power gives me exactly what He wants me to do at any given point in my recovery and, if I let Him, my willingness will bring Twelfth Step work automatically.

THINKING OF OTHERS

Our very lives, as ex-problem drinkers, depend upon our constant thought of others and how we may help meet their needs.

ALCOHOLICS ANONYMOUS, p. 20

Thinking of others has never come easily to me. Even when I try to work the A.A. program, I'm prone to thinking, "How do *I* feel today. Am *I* happy, joyous and free?"

The program tells me that my thoughts *must* reach out to those around me: "Would that newcomer welcome someone to talk to?" "That person looks a little unhappy today, maybe I could cheer him up." It is only when I forget my problems, and reach out to contribute something to others that I can begin to attain the serenity and God-consciousness I seek.

REACHING OUT

Never talk down to an alcoholic from any moral or spiritual hilltop; simply lay out the kit of spiritual tools for his inspection. Show him how they worked with you.

ALCOHOLICS ANONYMOUS, p. 95

When I come into contact with a newcomer, do I have a tendency to look at him from my perceived angle of success in A.A.? Do I compare him with the large number of acquaintances I have made in the Fellowship? Do I point out to him in a magisterial way the voice of A.A.? What is my *real* attitude toward him? I must examine myself whenever I meet a newcomer to make sure that I am carrying the message with simplicity, humility and generosity. The one who still suffers from the terrible disease of alcoholism must find in me a friend who will allow him to get to know the A.A. way, because I had such a friend when I arrived in A.A. Today it is my turn to hold out my hand, with love, to my sister or brother alcoholic, and to show her or him the way to happiness.

DOING ANYTHING TO HELP

Offer him [the alcoholic] friendship and fellowship. Tell him that if he wants to get well you will do anything to help.

ALCOHOLICS ANONYMOUS, p. 95

I remember how attracted I was to the two men from A.A. who Twelfth-Stepped me. They said I could have what they had, with no conditions attached, that all I had to do was make my own decision to join them on the pathway to recovery. When I start convincing a newcomer to do things my way, I forget how helpful those two men were to me in their open-minded generosity.

PARTNERS IN RECOVERY

. . . nothing will so much insure immunity from drinking as intensive work with other alcoholics. . . . Both you and the new man must walk day by day in the path of spiritual progress. . . . Follow the dictates of a Higher Power and you will presently live in a new and wonderful world, no matter what your present circumstances!

ALCOHOLICS ANONYMOUS, pp. 89, 100

Doing the right things for the right reasons—this is my way of controling my selfishness and self-centeredness. I realize that my dependency on a Higher Power clears the way for peace of mind, happiness and sobriety. I pray each day that I will avoid my previous actions, so that I will be helpful to others.

A PRICELESS REWARD

. . . work with other alcoholics. . . . It works when other activities fail.

ALCOHOLICS ANONYMOUS, p. 89

"Life will take on new meaning," as the Big Book says (p. 89). This promise has helped me to avoid self-seeking and self-pity. To watch others grow in this wonderful program, to see them improve the quality of their lives, is a priceless reward for my effort to help others. Self-examination is yet another reward for an ongoing recovery, as are serenity, peace and contentment. The energy derived from seeing others on a successful path, of sharing with them the joys of the journey, gives to my life a new meaning.

HONESTY WITH NEWCOMERS

Tell him exactly what happened to you. *Stress the spiritual feature freely.*

ALCOHOLICS ANONYMOUS, p. 93

The marvel of A.A. is that I tell only what happened to me. I don't waste time offering advice to potential newcomers, for if advice worked, nobody would get to A.A. All I have to do is show what has brought me sobriety and what has changed my life. If I fail to stress the spiritual feature of A.A.'s program, I am being dishonest. The newcomer should not be given a false impression of sobriety. I am sober only through the grace of my Higher Power, and that makes it possible for me to share with others.

UNDERSTANDING THE MALADY

When dealing with an alcoholic, there may be a natural annoyance that a man could be so weak, stupid and irresponsible. Even when you understand the malady better, you may feel this feeling rising.
ALCOHOLICS ANONYMOUS, p. 139

Having suffered from alcoholism, I should understand the illness, but sometimes I feel annoyance, even contempt, toward a person who cannot make it in A.A. When I feel that way, I am satisfying my false sense of superiority and I must remember, but for the grace of God, there go I.

THE REWARDS OF GIVING

This is indeed the kind of giving that actually demands nothing. He does not expect his brother sufferer to pay him, or even to love him. And then he discovers that by the divine paradox of this kind of giving he has found his own reward, whether his brother has yet received anything or not.

TWELVE STEPS AND TWELVE TRADITIONS, p. 109

Through experience with Twelfth Step work, I came to understand the rewards of giving that demands nothing in return. At first I expected recovery in others, but I soon learned that this did not happen. Once I acquired the humility to accept the fact that every Twelfth Step call was not going to result in a success, then I was open to receive the rewards of selfless giving.

LISTEN, SHARE AND PRAY

When working with a man and his family, you should take care not to participate in their quarrels. You may spoil your chance of being helpful if you do.
ALCOHOLICS ANONYMOUS, p. 100

When trying to help a fellow alcoholic, I've given in to an impulse to give advice, and perhaps that's inevitable. But allowing others the right to be wrong reaps its own benefits. The best I can do—and it sounds easier than it is to put into practice—is to listen, share personal experience, and pray for others.

PRINCIPLES, NOT PERSONALITIES

The way our "worthy" alcoholics have sometimes tried to judge the "less worthy" is, as we look back on it, rather comical. Imagine, if you can, one alcoholic judging another!
THE LANGUAGE OF THE HEART, p. 37

Who am I to judge anyone? When I first entered the Fellowship I found that I liked everyone. After all, A.A. was going to help me to a better way of life without alcohol. The reality was that I couldn't possibly like everyone, nor they me. As I've grown in the Fellowship, I've learned to love everyone just from listening to what they had to say. That person over there, or the one right here, may be the one God has chosen to give me the message I need for today. I must always remember to place principles above personalities.

RECOVERY, UNITY, SERVICE

Our Twelfth Step—carrying the message—is the basic service that AA's Fellowship gives; this is our principal aim and the main reason for our existence.
THE LANGUAGE OF THE HEART, p. 160

I thank God for those who came before me, those who told me not to forget the Three Legacies: Recovery, Unity and Service. In my home group, the Three Legacies were described on a sign which said: "You take a three-legged stool, try to balance it on only one leg, or two. Our Three Legacies must be kept intact. In Recovery, we get sober together; in Unity, we work together for the good of our Steps and Traditions; and through Service—we give away freely what has been given to us."

One of the chief gifts of my life has been to know that I will have no message to give, unless I recover in unity with A.A. principles.

A "SANE AND HAPPY USEFULNESS"

We have come to believe He would like us to keep our heads in the clouds with Him, but that our feet ought to be firmly planted on earth. That is where our fellow travelers are, and that is where our work must be done. These are the realities for us. We have found nothing incompatible between a powerful spiritual experience and a life of sane and happy usefulness.

ALCOHOLICS ANONYMOUS, p. 130

All the prayer and meditation in the world will not help me unless they are accompanied by action. Practicing the principles in all my affairs shows me the care that God takes in all parts of my life. God appears in my world when I move aside, and allow Him to step into it.

AT PEACE WITH LIFE

Every day is a day when we must carry the vision of God's will into all of our activities. "How can I best serve Thee—Thy will (not mine) be done."

ALCOHOLICS ANONYMOUS, p. 85

I read this passage each morning, to start off my day, because it is a continual reminder to "practice these principles in all my affairs." When I keep God's will at the forefront of my mind, I am able to do what I *should* be doing, and that puts me at peace with life, with myself and with God.

ACCEPTING SUCCESS OR FAILURE

Furthermore, how shall we come to terms with seeming failure or success? Can we now accept and adjust to either without despair or pride? Can we accept poverty, sickness, loneliness, and bereavement with courage and serenity? Can we steadfastly content ourselves with the humbler, yet sometimes more durable, satisfactions when the brighter, more glittering achievements are denied us?

TWELVE STEPS AND TWELVE TRADITIONS, p. 112

After I found A.A. and stopped drinking, it took a while before I understood why the First Step contained two parts: my powerlessness over alcohol, and my life's unmanageability. In the same way, I believed for a long time that, in order to be in tune with the Twelve Steps, it was enough for me "to carry this message to alcoholics." That was rushing things. I was forgetting that there were a total of Twelve Steps and that the Twelfth Step also had more than one part. Eventually I learned that it was necessary for me to "practice these principles" in all areas of my life. In working all the Steps thoroughly, I not only stay sober and help someone else to achieve sobriety, but also I transform my difficulty with living into a joy of living.

PROBLEM SOLVING

"Quite as important was the discovery that spiritual principles would solve all my problems."

ALCOHOLICS ANONYMOUS, p. 42

Through the recovery process described in the Big Book, I have come to realize that the same instructions that work on my alcoholism, work on much more. Whenever I am angry or frustrated, I consider the matter a manifestation of the main problem within me, alcoholism. As I "walk" through the Steps, my difficulty is usually dealt with long before I reach the Twelfth "suggestion," and those difficulties that persist are remedied when I make an effort to carry the message to someone else. These principles do solve my problems! I have not encountered an exception, and I have been brought to a way of living which is satisfying and useful.

SUIT UP AND SHOW UP

In A.A. we aim not only for sobriety—we try again to become citizens of the world that we rejected, and of the world that once rejected us. This is the ultimate demonstration toward which Twelfth Step work is the first but not the final step.

AS BILL SEES IT, p. 21

The old line says, "Suit up and show up." That action is so important that I like to think of it as my motto. I can choose each day to suit up and show up, or not. Showing up at meetings starts me toward feeling a part of that meeting, for then I can do what I say I'll do at meetings. I can talk with newcomers, and I can share my experience; that's what credibility, honesty, and courtesy really are. Suiting up and showing up are the concrete actions I take in my ongoing return to normal living.

THE JOY OF LIVING

. . . therefore the joy of good living is the theme of A.A.'s Twelfth Step.
TWELVE STEPS AND TWELVE TRADITIONS, p 125

A.A. *is* a joyful program! Even so, I occasionally balk at taking the necessary steps to move ahead, and find myself resisting the very actions that could bring about the joy I want. I would not resist if those actions did not touch some vulnerable area of my life, an area that needs hope and fulfillment. Repeated exposure to joyfulness has a way of softening the hard, outer edges of my ego. Therein lies the power of joyfulness to help all members of A.A.

ANONYMITY

Anonymity is the spiritual foundation of our Traditions, ever reminding us to place principles before personalities.

ALCOHOLICS ANONYMOUS, p. 564

Tradition Twelve became important early in my sobriety and, along with the Twelve Steps, it continues to be a must in my recovery. I became aware after I joined the Fellowship that I had personality problems, so that when I first heard it, the Tradition's message was very clear: there exists an immediate way for me to face, with others, my alcoholism and attendant anger, defensiveness, offensiveness. I saw Tradition Twelve as being a great ego-deflator; it relieved my anger and gave me a chance to utilize the principles of the program. All of the Steps, and this particular Tradition, have guided me over decades of continuous sobriety. I am grateful to those who were here when I needed them.

DAILY RESOLUTIONS

The idea of "twenty-four-hour living" applies primarily to the emotional life of the individual. Emotionally speaking, we must not live in yesterday, nor in tomorrow.

AS BILL SEES IT, p. 284

A New Year: 12 months, 52 weeks, 365 days, 8,760 hours, 525,600 minutes—a time to consider directions, goals, and actions. I must make some plans to live a normal life, but also I must live emotionally within a twenty-four-hour frame, for if I do, I don't have to make New Year's resolutions! I can make every day a New Year's day! I can decide, "Today I will do this . . . Today I will do that." Each day I can measure my life by trying to do a little better, by deciding to follow God's will and by making an effort to put the principles of our A.A. program into action.

THE TWELVE STEPS
OF ALCOHOLICS ANONYMOUS

1. We admitted we were powerless over alcohol—that our lives had become unmanageable.

2. Came to believe that a Power greater than ourselves could restore us to sanity.

3. Made a decision to turn our will and our lives over to the care of God *as we understood Him.*

4. Made a searching and fearless moral inventory of ourselves.

5. Admitted to God, to ourselves and to another human being the exact nature of our wrongs.

6. Were entirely ready to have God remove all these defects of character.

7. Humbly asked Him to remove our shortcomings.

8. Made a list of all persons we had harmed, and became willing to make amends to them all.

9. Made direct amends to such people wherever possible, except when to do so would injure them or others.

10. Continued to take personal inventory and when we were wrong promptly admitted it.

11. Sought through prayer and meditation to improve our conscious contact with God, *as we understood Him,* praying only for knowledge of His will for us and the power to carry that out.

12. Having had a spiritual awakening as the result of these steps, we tried to carry this message to alcoholics, and to practice these principles in all our affairs.

THE TWELVE TRADITIONS
OF ALCOHOLICS ANONYMOUS

1. Our common welfare should come first; personal recovery depends upon A.A. unity.

2. For our group purpose there is but one ultimate authority— a loving God as He may express Himself in our group conscience. Our leaders are but trusted servants; they do not govern.

3. The only requirement for A.A. membership is a desire to stop drinking.

4. Each group should be autonomous except in matters affecting other groups or A.A. as a whole.

5. Each group has but one primary purpose—to carry its message to the alcoholic who still suffers.

6. An A.A. group ought never endorse, finance, or lend the A.A. name to any related facility or outside enterprise, lest problems of money, property, and prestige divert us from our primary purpose.

7. Every A.A. group ought to be fully self-supporting, declining outside contributions.

8. Alcoholics Anonymous should remain forever non-professional, but our service centers may employ special workers.

9. A.A., as such, ought never be organized; but we may create service boards or committees directly responsible to those they serve.

10. Alcoholics Anonymous has no opinion on outside issues; hence the A.A. name ought never be drawn into public controversy.

11. Our public relations policy is based on attraction rather than promotion; we need always maintain personal anonymity at the level of press, radio, and films.

12. Anonymity is the spiritual foundation of all our traditions, ever reminding us to place principles before personalities.

INDEX